Leadership Lullabies

By: Mustafa Nejem

Foreword

Dear Children,

With sincere gratitude and joy, we welcome you to the exciting world of "Leadership Lullabies". Your decision to start this journey with us is our commitment to foster leadership qualities in a unique way to reach the hearts of the young dreamers.

We extend our heartfelt thanks for trusting us to be part of your bedtime routine, recognizing the profound impact of stories in shaping the minds of our future leaders.
We aspire to be an asset to your knowledge and the creative narratives that await your attention. By combining the magic of story-telling with interactive activities, we aim to provide not just a book but a mindful experience for our children!

Thank you for choosing "Leadership Lullabies" as a trusted friend in the essential journey of cultivating leadership in the hearts of those you cherish the most.

With gratitude and excitement,

Author, "Leadership Lullabies"

Table of Contents

Introduction

***

Welcome to the world of "Leadership Lullabies", a magical journey that is designed to inspire you and sow the seeds of leadership in the hearts of young and emerging minds! In these pages of the exciting and unique journey of leadership, the tales of Enchanted Forest bring forward the lessons of wisdom, courage, self-reflection, and creativity.

In the era of childhood, where imagination is limitless, we board on an extraordinary adventure with Luna, The Wise Owl, Buzz, The Brave Little Bee, Princess Harmony, Sir Determination, and many other delightful characters. Through their stories, we aim to plant the seeds of leadership, teaching our young readers essential values that will blossom into the qualities of compassionate and capable leaders.

"Leadership Lullabies" is not just a collection of bedtime stories but a mindful blend of entertainment and education. As you unfold the pages, you will come across the power of Princess Harmony's kingdom, the flexibility needed to face challenges with Sir Determination, and the importance of Little Giggle Goblins' playful gestures.

My children, the magic doesn't stop here! Part II of our book invites you all to enter the Land of games and activities. The Leadership Treasure Hunt, Storyboard Leadership, and The Great Leadership Bake-Off are just a few examples of the engaging experiences that await. By involving children in hands-on, collaborative endeavors, we aim to reinforce the lessons learned in the stories, making leadership principles tangible and applicable in their own lives.

We hope that this book serves not only as a delightful bedtime companion but also as a source of inspiration, sparking curiosity, creativity, and kindness in the hearts of our young leaders.

May the Enchanted Forest continue to live on in the dreams and aspirations of our little ones, reminding them of the magic within and the limitless possibilities that await as they embrace the journey of leadership.

Sweet dreams and magical adventures await you in the pages of "Leadership Lullabies."

Regards,
Author, Leadership Lullabies

Part I:
Bedtime Stories for Growing Great Leaders

The Enchanted Forest

Chapter 1

The Adventure Begins

***

In the heart of the Enchanted Forest, where moonbeams danced through the treetops, there lived Luna, an owl known for her extraordinary wisdom. As the silver moon cast its glow, Luna's eyes sparkled with knowledge that surpassed the ageless trees surrounding her.

In "The Wise Owl's Wisdom," is a magical journey with Luna, an owl whose feathers are adorned with the tales of countless adventures and the echoes of ancient wisdom.

Once upon a time, in the heart of the Enchanted Forest, where emerald leaves rustled with secrets and the air was filled with the sweet melody of hidden streams, there lived Luna, a wise and gentle owl with feathers as soft as moonlight.

Luna, often found perched atop the tallest tree, became known far and wide for her vast knowledge and wisdom. Her eyes, gleaming like twin stars in the night sky, held the stories of the ancient forest. Every creature, from the tiny fireflies to the majestic deer, sought Luna's counsel.

One evening, as the sun dipped below the horizon and the first stars began to twinkle, Luna sensed a gathering of curious animals below her tree. Sensing their eagerness to learn, Luna gracefully descended, her wings barely making a sound as she landed.

With a sparkle in her eyes, Luna began to share tales of the Enchanted Forest – stories of bravery, kindness, and the importance of understanding the language of the wind. Each word she uttered held the weight of centuries of wisdom, and the forest creatures listened in awe.

In Luna's imaginative narrative, the forest came alive with magical creatures and vibrant landscapes. The animals found themselves immersed in a world where trees whispered ancient secrets, and every rustle of the leaves held a hidden message. Luna, with her enchanting storytelling, painted a picture of a world where leadership was not about power but about understanding, about having the unique qualities of every creature in the forest.

As Luna spoke, a young bunny named Thistle found herself captivated by the tales of Luna's adventures. Luna noticed the sparkle of curiosity in Thistle's eyes and invited her to ask any question that fluttered in her heart.

Thistle hesitated for a moment before asking,

"How can I become a wise leader like you, Luna?"

Luna, with a gentle twinkle in her eyes, shared a piece of advice that would be of great help to every creature in the Enchanted Forest:

"Listen, dear Thistle, listen to the whispers of the trees, the laughter of the streams, and the stories carried by the wind. True wisdom lies not just in what you know but in your willingness to learn from the world around you."

From that day forward, Thistle and the other forest dwellers gathered under Luna's tree, eager to absorb the timeless wisdom she shared. Luna's imaginative narratives became a treasure trove of knowledge, shaping the young minds of the Enchanted Forest into compassionate and wise leaders.

And so, the tale of Luna, The Wise Owl, unfolded, leaving behind a legacy of leadership that sparkled like moonbeams in the hearts of all who listened. The Enchanted Forest became a place where wisdom flourished, and the stories of Luna echoed through the ages, carried by the wind to inspire generations of leaders yet to come.

In the heart of the Enchanted Forest, Luna, the wise owl, continued her nightly gatherings beneath the ancient tree. As the moon hung high, casting a silver glow upon the attentive assembly of creatures, Luna felt a profound responsibility to impart lessons that would shape not only the minds but also the hearts of those who gathered beneath her.

On one such evening, the air was filled with anticipation as Luna's feathers rustled with a tale of great significance. Luna began to weave a story, not just with words, but with the essence of wisdom that permeated the very air around her.

"Dear friends," Luna began, her voice a soothing melody, "Leadership, like the ebb and flow of the forest stream, requires a skill often overlooked but immensely powerful – the art of attentive listening."

As Luna's words danced through the air, every creature, from the smallest squirrel to the wisest old tortoise, sat in rapt attention, their eyes fixed upon Luna's wise gaze.

"In the symphony of the Enchanted Forest, every rustle, every chirp, and every whisper holds a lesson," Luna continued.

"True leaders understand the importance of not only speaking but, more importantly, listening. Attentive listening is like opening your heart to the stories of others, embracing the wisdom that surrounds you."

Luna's words lingered in the air, sinking into the hearts of her enchanted audience. She illustrated the concept with a tale of two songbirds, each with a unique melody to share. The wise leaders of

the forest, she explained, would sit in silence, absorbing the diverse tunes, recognizing that the richness of the symphony lay in the harmonious interplay of every note.

The young creatures in the assembly exchanged knowing glances, understanding that Luna's lesson transcended the realm of the Enchanted Forest and echoed into the very fabric of leadership in their lives.

"To lead with wisdom is to listen with an open heart," Luna concluded. "For in the quiet moments of attentive listening, we find the threads of unity, understanding, and shared purpose."

As Luna's words faded into the night, the creatures of the Enchanted Forest embraced the profound lesson of attentive listening. From that moment on, the forest resounded with a harmony born not only from the melodies of nature but from the deep understanding that every voice, no matter how small, played a crucial part in the grand leadership.

And so, Luna, the wise owl, continued to illuminate the path for her fellow creatures, leaving them with the enduring wisdom that, in the stillness of attentive listening, the true magic of leadership unfolded.

Chapter 2

The Brave Little Bee
***

In the Enchanted Forest, where the emerald canopies met in a dance with the gentle breeze, a unique character named Buzz, The Brave Little Bee, buzzed with an unyielding spirit that resonated throughout the Golden Meadows. This extraordinary meadow, bathed in the golden hues of the sun, was home to an array of magical creatures who lived in harmony under the watchful gaze of the ancient trees.

One day, a gentle whisper rustled through the leaves, announcing the arrival of a unique challenge that stirred excitement and curiosity in the hearts of the enchanted beings. The Golden Meadows were graced with the presence of a mystical portal, a shimmering gateway to the unknown. The meadow dwellers gathered, their eyes filled with a mixture of anticipation and anxiety.

Buzz, with his distinctive yellow and black stripes, stood at the forefront. His small but determined stature radiated courage that inspired his fellow creatures. As the appointed leader, Buzz felt a responsibility to guide his friends through the new areas that lay beyond the portal.

With a rallying buzz that echoed through the meadow, Buzz spoke,

"Dear friends, our Golden Meadows have bestowed upon us a challenge, a journey into the unknown. But fear not, for we shall face this adventure together. It is in unity that our strength lies."

The enchanted beings, from the wise old owls to the playful pixies, nodded in agreement. The importance of group leadership became evident as Buzz emphasized the need for every creature to contribute their unique strengths to overcome the challenges ahead.

As they approached the mystical portal, a shimmering veil that seemed to hum with ancient secrets, a hush fell over the meadow. Buzz, with a deep breath and unwavering resolve, took the lead. The courage he displayed ignited a spark within the hearts of his fellow meadow dwellers.

Through the portal, the characters entered a realm of swirling colors and mesmerizing landscapes. Challenges awaited them at every turn, from enchanted puzzles that tested their wit to mysterious creatures that required collaboration to overcome. The Golden Meadows inhabitants faced the unknown with a shared courage that mirrored the bravery of their leader, Buzz.

Emphasizing the importance of courage in leadership, Buzz and his companions encountered moments of uncertainty and awe-inspiring beauty. The journey forged bonds among them, turning a diverse group of creatures into a formidable team, each contributing their unique strengths to overcome the challenges of the mystical realm.

As they emerged on the other side of the portal, the meadow dwellers carried with them not only the treasures they had gathered but also the invaluable lessons of group leadership and the unyielding courage needed to face the unknown.

The Golden Meadows, now more enchanted than ever, whispered tales of their adventure, a testament to the bravery and unity that blossomed under Buzz's guidance.

And so, Buzz, The Brave Little Bee, became a symbol in the Enchanted Forest, a reminder that in facing the unknown, the strength of a leader lies not just in personal courage but in the collective bravery of those who journey together.

As the Golden Meadows basked in the warm glow of the setting sun, Buzz, The Brave Little Bee, became a living legend among the meadow dwellers. The tales of his leadership and the journey through the mystical portal resonated in every petal and leaf. Yet, Buzz knew that their adventure was not merely a story to be told but a transformative experience that held profound lessons for the entire Enchanted Forest.

Word spread through the meadow, reaching the ears of creatures both near and far. The enchanted beings, drawn by the allure of the Golden Meadows and the tales of courage, gathered to hear Buzz share the wisdom gained from their extraordinary journey.

Perched on a blossom-covered stage, Buzz addressed the eager assembly.

"Dear friends, our journey through the mystical portal was not just a quest for treasures but a testament to the power of courage and resilience in leadership. Our challenges and trials were not merely obstacles but metaphors for the adversities leaders may encounter in their journeys."

With a captivating buzz, Buzz recounted the moments when the path through the mystical realm seemed shrouded in uncertainty. Some puzzles tested the limits of their wit, creatures that challenged their resolve, and landscapes that demanded resilience. Buzz emphasized how, in those trying moments, leadership was not about avoiding challenges but facing them with unwavering determination.

"Leadership," Buzz declared, "is a journey where every trial, every setback, is an opportunity to grow stronger. It's about facing the unknown with the resilience of a blooming flower after a storm. The challenges we encountered were not meant to break us but to shape us into leaders who can weather any storm."

The meadow dwellers listened intently, their eyes reflecting a shared understanding of the profound lessons Buzz imparted. His words echoed in their hearts, becoming a source of inspiration for every creature, young and old.

In the days that followed, the Enchanted Forest saw a transformative ripple effect. Buzz's tale became a guiding light for leaders of various species, from the soaring eagles to the burrowing badgers. The importance of facing challenges with courage and resilience resonated across the meadow, fostering a spirit of determination that permeated every corner of the Golden Meadows.

As Buzz continued to lead, his bravery and determination inspired others to discover their inner strength. The once-unknown portal became a symbol of endless possibilities and the challenges it held transformed into stepping stones for leaders to rise above adversity.

Buzz's wings, once tested in the mystical kingdom, now fluttered with newfound strength, carrying the echoes of his bravery to every corner of the enchanted realm. The Enchanted Forest, forever changed by Buzz's leadership, embraced a future where courage and resilience were the guiding forces, ensuring that challenges would be faced not with fear but with the unwavering spirit of a Brave Little Bee.

Chapter 3

Princess Harmony and
the Kingdom of Empathy
***

In the Enchanted Forest, where the gentle glow of fairy lights danced through the leaves, Princess Harmony reigned over the magical kingdom of Empathica. Her presence alone emanated a soothing aura, and her every step left traces of kindness in the air. Empathica, a realm nestled between towering trees adorned with iridescent leaves, was a haven where creatures of all shapes and sizes coexisted in harmony.

One day, as the sun dipped below the horizon, Princess Harmony gathered the enchanted beings in a moonlit clearing, the air tinged with the fragrance of blooming flowers. With a voice as melodious as the woodland symphony, she began to share the wisdom of empathy.

"Dear friends,"

Harmony spoke,

"In Empathica, empathy is our guiding principle. The magical force connects us all, fostering a deep understanding of each other's feelings and experiences."

In the center of the clearing, Princess Harmony conjured heart-shaped pendants, each infused with a unique color that shimmered like the hues of a mesmerizing sunset. The pendants sparkled with an ethereal glow, reflecting the emotional tapestry they would soon weave.

"These heart-shaped pendants are more than just jewelry,"

Harmony explained. "They are tokens of our shared connection through empathy. Wear them with pride, for they symbolize the invisible threads that bind our hearts, creating a tapestry of unity and compassion."

As Princess Harmony distributed the pendants, the enchanted beings felt a warm energy enveloping them. The colors of the pendants resonated with their emotions, creating a beautiful dance of lights in the moonlit clearing. The air became charged with a shared understanding, and the creatures of Empathica felt a newfound closeness.

In the days that followed, the transformative power of empathy unfolded in Empathica. The enchanted beings, guided by the shared connection represented by their heart-shaped pendants, began to approach one another with open hearts and open minds. They listened deeply, sought to understand, and embraced the emotions of their fellow creatures.

One evening, a wise old tortoise named Terra approached Princess Harmony, his heart-shaped pendant gleaming with a warm, earthy glow. He shared a tale of a younger creature, Sparkle the Fairy, who was struggling with feelings of loneliness.

Princess Harmony, with her heart-shaped pendant radiating a soft, empathic light, gathered the community to support Sparkle. Together, they organized a moonlit gathering, where Sparkle felt heard, understood, and surrounded by the warmth of empathy. It became a powerful lesson for everyone in Empathica—the ability to share and embrace each other's emotions strengthened the bonds of the community.

As time passed, the enchanted beings of Empathica realized that empathy wasn't just a magical element of their kingdom but a life-enhancing force. Princess Harmony's leadership, rooted in empathy, had transformed Empathica into a realm where understanding and compassion flourished.

The heart-shaped pendants, now glowing brightly on every enchanted being, became a constant reminder of their shared connection through empathy. The Enchanted Forest echoed with tales of harmony and unity, and Princess Harmony's lessons lived on as a testament to the enduring magic that blossomed when hearts were connected through empathy. In Empathica, the wisdom of Princess Harmony had not only transformed a kingdom but had sown seeds of empathy that would ripple through the Enchanted Forest for generations to come.

66

Hush, little one, close your eyes,

Stars are twinkling in the skies.

Moonlight whispers, soft and low,

Dreamland's calling, off you go.

Sleep, my dear, in tender grace,

Moonbeams gently touch your face.

As the night unfolds its charms,
Drift away in sleepy arms.

99

Chapter **4**

The Kindness Castle
✳✳✳

The sunlight filtered through the leaves in a kaleidoscope of colors; there stood the Kindness Castle—an enchanting kingdom dedicated to the extraordinary power of kindness. This magical abode was not just a fortress of stone but a living testament to the importance of compassion and warmth in leadership.

Within the walls of the Kindness Castle, each stone radiated a gentle glow, and the air hummed with the harmonious tunes of kindness. The castle was ruled by Queen Serenity, a benevolent leader whose heart brimmed with kindness that touched every corner of the Enchanted Forest.

One bright morning, Queen Serenity gathered the enchanted beings in the castle courtyard. The whimsical creatures of the forest, from the mischievous sprites to the majestic unicorns, eagerly awaited the queen's wise words.

"My dear friends," Queen Serenity began her voice like a soothing melody, "kindness is the true magic that binds us all. It is not just a gesture but a force that can transform the world around us."

As Queen Serenity spoke, the Kindness Castle came alive with magical elements. The stones shimmered with ethereal hues, and colourful butterflies danced in the air, creating an enchanting atmosphere that captivated the enchanted beings.

To illustrate the importance of kindness in leadership, Queen Serenity decided to bestow a special gift upon each creature in the courtyard. With a wave of her hand, she conjured the Kindness Crown—a delicate tiara adorned with blossoming flowers and sparkling gems.

"These Kindness Crowns," Queen Serenity explained, "are symbols of your commitment to leadership through kindness. Wear them with pride, for they signify your role in promoting compassion and warmth within our Enchanted Forest."

The enchanted beings, with gratitude in their hearts, accepted the Kindness Crowns. The crowns glowed with a soft light, reflecting the kindness within each creature. The air buzzed with anticipation as the creatures embraced their newfound responsibility.

In the days that followed, the Kindness Castle became a hub of heartwarming activities. Queen Serenity and her subjects embarked on quests to spread kindness throughout the Enchanted Forest. From helping a lost bunny find its way home to planting seeds of friendship between feuding sprites, the creatures discovered that even the smallest acts of kindness could create ripples of joy.

One day, a curious pixie named Twinkle found herself in a dilemma. She had accidentally scattered a basket of colourful feathers belonging to Sparkle, the carefree rainbow-hued parrot. The courtyard fell silent, awaiting Twinkle's fate.

Queen Serenity, donning her own Kindness Crown, approached Twinkle with a warm smile. Instead of scolding the pixie, she offered a helping hand to gather the feathers. The magical atmosphere in the Kindness Castle intensified as the creatures witnessed the transformative power of kindness in leadership.

As a reward for Queen Serenity's act of kindness, the enchanted beings, one by one, began to spontaneously burst into cheerful songs, filling the Kindness Castle with a symphony of joy. The air was alive with the magic of shared kindness, and the Kindness Crowns glowed brighter than ever.

The lesson learned within the walls of the Kindness Castle echoed through the Enchanted Forest. The enchanted beings, crowned with kindness, became leaders in promoting compassion and warmth. The Kindness Castle stood not only as a symbol of benevolent leadership but as a beacon of hope, reminding all who passed by that kindness had the power to create a world where hearts were connected and joy flourished in abundance.

The lesson became crystal clear—the transformative power of kindness in leadership was not about avoiding mistakes but about responding with empathy and understanding. Queen Serenity's act of kindness sparked a chain reaction. The creatures, inspired by her example, began to spontaneously burst into cheerful songs, creating a symphony of joy that echoed through the Enchanted Forest.

The Kindness Castle, now an ideal of benevolent leadership, stood as evidence of the enduring magic of kindness. The enchanted beings, crowned with the Kindness Crowns, discovered that leadership was not about wielding power but about creating a world where hearts were connected, and joy flourished in abundance. The lesson learned within the walls of the Kindness Castle echoed through the Enchanted Forest, leaving an indelible mark on the hearts of its enchanted inhabitants for generations to come.

Chapter 5

Sir Determination and
the Dragon of Challenges
***

The ancient trees stood tall and proud and lived Sir Determination, a noble knight whose spirit burned with an unyielding flame. The Enchanted Forest, though magical, was not immune to challenges, and its inhabitants often faced obstacles that tested their resolve. Sir Determination, with his gleaming armor and unwavering gaze, became a symbol of perseverance in the face of adversity.

One day, a shadow loomed over the Enchanted Forest—a colossal dragon named Obstacleus, the Dragon of Challenges. Its scales shimmered with the sorts of difficulties that creatures faced, and its fiery breath symbolized the trials that tested the courage of those who dared to venture through the forest.

News of the dragon's presence spread, and a hushed murmur filled the enchanted glades. Sir Determination, ever vigilant, felt a surge of determination within him. It was time to face the Dragon of Challenges and teach the enchanted beings the invaluable lesson of perseverance.

As Sir Determination approached the dragon's lair, the air crackled with tension. The forest stood still, awaiting the epic battle that would unfold. The knight faced Obstacleus, its eyes glinting with the reflections of countless challenges it had posed to the forest inhabitants.

With a resounding battle cry, Sir Determination charged towards the dragon, his armor clinking with each step. The dragon unleashed torrents of fiery challenges—obstacles that seemed insurmountable. Yet, Sir Determination, fueled by his unyielding spirit, dodged and parried each challenge with skill and determination.

The battle raged on, and the Enchanted Forest watched in awe as Sir Determination confronted the Dragon of Challenges with an unwavering positive mindset. His sword, named Perseverance, gleamed as he struck blow after blow, not just at the dragon's physical form but at the very essence of the challenges it represented.

During the fierce battle, Sir Determination found himself faced with a particularly daunting obstacle— a wall of doubt conjured by the dragon. The enchanted beings held their breath as the knight, with a determined spark in his eyes, raised his shield of Optimism. The wall crumbled with a *crash*, revealing the dragon vulnerable to the resilience of a positive mindset.

Next, he navigated the treacherous Swamp of Setbacks, where each step seemed to lead him deeper into the murky waters of setbacks. Undeterred, Sir Determination pressed on, his armour gleaming with the resilience that came from facing challenges head-on.

The final leg of his journey led him to the Whispering Woods, where shadows of fear and whispers of failure tested his resolve. With a heart unyielding, Sir Determination faced the haunting echoes, turning them into a masterpiece of courage that echoed through the Enchanted Forest.

With each conquered challenge, Sir Determination grew stronger, and the Dragon of Challenges weakened. The Enchanted Forest, witnessing the knight's unwavering spirit, resonated with the triumphant *roar* of the Dragon of Challenges as it succumbed to Sir Determination's indomitable will.

The Enchanted Forest erupted in cheers as obstacles dissipated like morning mist. Sir Determination, though weary, stood victorious. The enchanted beings, inspired by his resilience, crowned him the Hero of Hope.

With one final, mighty swing, Sir Determination struck the decisive blow. The Dragon of Challenges, its fiery form now diminished, let out a defeated *hiss*. The Enchanted Forest erupted in cheers as obstacles dissipated like morning mist.

The lesson echoed through the forest—a positive mindset, coupled with perseverance, could triumph over even the most formidable challenges. Sir Determination, panting but victorious, stood before the enchanted beings, his armor slightly tarnished but his spirit unbroken.

> *"Dear friends," Sir Determination proclaimed, "the Dragon of Challenges may loom large, but with determination and a positive mindset, no obstacle is insurmountable. Each challenge is an opportunity for growth and victory."*

The Enchanted Forest, now free from the shadows of doubt, embraced the lesson taught by Sir Determination. The knight became a living legend, a symbol of resilience and the indomitable human spirit. Obstacleus, once a fearsome adversary, transformed into a reminder that challenges, when faced with determination and optimism, could be conquered.

And so, Sir Determination continued to roam the Enchanted Forest, his tale inspiring generations to come. The Dragon of Challenges, now a distant memory, left in its wake a legacy of perseverance and the enduring belief that, with the right mindset, every obstacle could be transformed into a stepping stone toward a brighter, more resilient future. The forest resounded with the *applause* of leaves as the creatures celebrated the victory.

Chapter 6

The Magical Mirror
of Self-Reflection
***

It was a bright, sunny morning in the lush Enchanted Forest. Luna the Wise Old Owl fluttered between the towering oak and ash trees, their ancient branches swaying gently in the breeze. Colourful birds sang sweet songs as they flitted among the leaves.

Luna had lived many long years in these woods and seen much. But rumors had reached her large pointed ears of a most curious sight deep in the forest - a magical mirror said to reveal mysteries of the soul. Luna's owl eyes, wise and amber, were keen to investigate this wonder.

She flew on softly between the trees, gazing around with her keen vision.

"Mirror, mirror, where have you been hiding?" Luna hooted softly.

She searched for some time, peering beneath fallen logs and into moss-covered hollows. Just as she was about to give up her search, Luna spotted a glow up ahead through the dense forest.

She fluttered toward the silvery light and emerged into a sun-dappled clearing. Here stood an ornate full-length mirror atop a circular marble pedestal, emanating a soft radiance. Beside it flew Buzz the Brave Little Bee, buzzing with excitement.

Though small, Buzz was never afraid to explore. He had often ventured into dangerous storm clouds to pollinate flowers or dived into rushing rivers to rescue drowning insects. But even he felt a tingle of awe before the mirror's magic.

Just then, Princess Harmony rode into view upon her noble white pony, Twinkles. Her long pink hair flowed behind her in the gentle breeze, and her smile was as warm and bright as the sunny glade.

"Greetings, friends, I've come to see this mirror of the legend you spoke of," said Harmony kindly. She dismounted and joined Luna and Buzz before the looking glass.

The three gazed deep into its silvery depths, enchanted. Slowly, scenes began to form within the mirror's shining surface...

Luna saw herself perched high in an oak during a snowstorm, guiding a lost fox pup back to its den with her wise directions. She realized the insights and advice she had imparted to all the creatures of the forest over her long life.

Buzz witnessed diving fearlessly into a raging beehive to rescue a honeybee trapped within. Though his tiny body trembled, his courage and heart of gold never faltered.

Harmony beheld times of bringing enemies together in council, finding peaceful compromises through calm discussion, and care for all. Her reign had brought prosperity through compassion.

Yet shadows crept in the reflections, too, revealing doubts... Times Luna wondered if she truly knew the right path, challenges that tested Buzz's bravery to its limits, waves of uncertainty beneath Harmony's kind rule.

The friends shared their new understandings in hushed, thoughtful tones. For Luna, embracing both certainty and self-doubt strengthened her wisdom. Buzz recognized facing fear head-on was the truest courage. Harmony realized leadership lay not in being flawless but in following one's caring heart.

Inspired by this newfound awareness, the trio began to share their reflections. Laughter echoed through the clearing, empathy flowed like a gentle stream, and mutual understanding blossomed like the enchanting flowers that surrounded them. The Mirror of Reflection, delighted by the harmony it had fostered, shimmered with approval.

The lesson learned was profound: self-reflection and self-awareness are the foundations of growth and effective leadership. Accepting one's strengths and vulnerabilities allows for genuine connections with others and inspires collective growth.

As the enchanted beings left the clearing, the Mirror of Reflection continued to radiate its magical glow. The story of the mirror's transformative powers spread like wildfire through the Enchanted Forest, encouraging all its inhabitants to embrace the enchanting journey of self-discovery. The lesson, wrapped in the simplicity of understanding oneself, became a guiding light for generations to come—a reminder that true leadership begins with knowing and accepting the magic within.

And so, the Mirror of Reflection stood as a timeless testament to the transformative power of self-awareness in the heart of the Enchanted Forest, continuing to weave its enchanting tales for those who dared to gaze into its depths.

As they left the glade, changed but wiser within, the Mirror of Reflection's magic shimmered - that self-reflection nourishes leadership by cultivating self-awareness through sharing both light and shadow within. Its glow remains as a reminder in the heart of the Enchanted Forest.

Chapter 7

The Giggle Goblins' Lesson

***

Once upon a time, in the Enchanted Forest, where the trees whispered secrets and the flowers giggled in the moonlight, lived three extraordinary creatures known as the Giggle Goblins: Giggly, Chuckle, and Snicker.

Giggly, with his vibrant purple fur and a perpetually gleeful expression, was the leader of the trio. His infectious laughter could turn even the gloomiest day into a carnival of joy. Giggly's humour was characterized by whimsical tales and playful pranks. His jokes were like a burst of confetti, leaving a trail of mirth wherever he went.

Chuckle, the second in command, was a rotund Giggle Goblin with a green polka-dotted coat that jingled with every step. Chuckle's style of humour was all about witty remarks and clever wordplay. His laugh resembled the rhythmic chiming of a thousand bells, creating a symphony of amusement that echoed through the Enchanted Forest.

Last but not least was Snicker, the mischievous prankster of the trio. Snicker's fur was a dazzling shade of blue, and his eyes sparkled with a twinkle of mischief. He had an uncanny ability to find humour in the most unexpected places, turning even the most mundane situations into uproarious comedy. Snicker's laughter, a series of high-pitched snickers, was like a magical melody that enchanted everyone around him.

One sunny day in the Enchanted Forest, the Giggle Goblins were called upon by the wise Old Oak, the oldest and most respected tree in the forest, to help lift the spirits of the woodland creatures. The normally cheerful creatures were feeling downhearted due to the arrival of the dreary Rainclouds that threatened to spoil their joy.

Giggly, Chuckle, and Snicker sprang into action of laughter that would shoo away the Rainclouds and bring back the sunshine. Giggly started with his tales of magical tickleberries that made everyone laugh uncontrollably, while Chuckle sprinkled puns and jokes like fairy dust, creating a carnival of chuckles.

Snicker, being the master of surprises, orchestrated a series of whimsical pranks that had everyone, from the wise Old Oak to the tiniest woodland creature, bursting into fits of giggles. As the laughter echoed through the Enchanted Forest, the Rainclouds couldn't resist the infectious joy, and one by one, they dissipated into a burst of rainbow confetti.

The woodland creatures, now bathed in the warm glow of happiness, cheered for the Giggle Goblins.

 The Old Oak, with a voice like rustling leaves, spoke,

"Giggly, Chuckle, and Snicker, your laughter has saved the day and brought light to our Enchanted Forest. You've shown us the power of joy, even in the face of gloom. Your unique styles of humour have reminded us that laughter is the key to unlocking the magic within."

And so, the Giggle Goblins, with their vibrant personalities and contagious laughter, became the guardians of laughter in the Enchanted Forest, spreading joy and positivity wherever they went. The creatures of the forest, inspired by their example, learned to find humour in every situation, and the Enchanted Forest echoed with laughter for generations to come.

One day, Giggly, Chuckle, and Snicker decided to organize a grand laughter festival like the Enchanted Forest. They called it the "Giggle Gala," a magical event filled with playful challenges and whimsical competitions to spread joy far and wide.

To kick off the festivities, Giggly proposed the "Tickleberry Toss," where participants had to toss berries at each other, and the first to burst into laughter would be declared the winner. Chuckle, with his witty remarks, hosted the "Pun Parade," where contestants had to come up with the silliest puns, and the audience roared with laughter at each clever wordplay.

Meanwhile, Snicker orchestrated the "Prankster's Relay," a race filled with magical pranks and surprises. Participants had to navigate through a field of invisible tickle traps and slippery banana peels, creating a symphony of snickers as they stumbled and giggled their way to the finish line.

The Giggle Gala wasn't just about laughter; it was infused with enchanting elements to make it a truly magical experience. Colourful butterflies fluttered around, casting spells of joy with every flap of their wings. The trees themselves seemed to chuckle, their leaves rustling in amusement as the Giggle Goblins showcased their playful leadership.

As the day unfolded, the woodland creatures embraced the challenges with enthusiasm, realizing that laughter could turn even the simplest tasks into delightful adventures. The positive energy radiating from the Giggle Gala began to transform the Enchanted Forest. Flowers bloomed with brighter colors, and the air was filled with the sweet fragrance of laughter.

Amid the festivities, the wise Old Oak made a surprise appearance. "Giggly, Chuckle, and Snicker," the Old Oak boomed,

> *"You have not only brought laughter to our forest but have shown us the true power of a positive attitude. Leadership is not just about making decisions; it's about inspiring others, and you've done so with joy and creativity."*

The Giggle Goblins, surrounded by a sea of smiling faces, felt a sense of accomplishment. The playful challenges and magical elements not only entertained but also taught the importance of embracing positivity in leadership roles. The young readers, captivated by the enchanting narrative, couldn't help but carry away the lesson that a positive attitude can be a powerful and transformative force in any leadership journey.

As the Giggle Gala concluded with a spectacular display of fireworks shaped like laughter bubbles, the Enchanted Forest glowed with a newfound radiance. The Giggle Goblins, their hearts brimming with joy, continued to lead with laughter, leaving a legacy of positivity.

Chapter **8**

King Creativity's Canvas

In the core of the Enchanted Forest, nestled the towering trees and shimmering streams, stood King Creativity's Workshop, a hub of innovation where ideas came to life. Luna, the wise owl, had heard whispers about this magical place, and she knew it was time to introduce her young friends to the wonders of creativity.

Gathering the enchanted creatures—Thistle the bunny, Buzz the brave little bee, and a host of other curious beings—Luna embarked on a journey to King Creativity's Workshop. As they approached the workshop, a vibrant energy filled the air, and the sound of laughter and tinkling tools filled their ears.

The workshop was a haven of inspiration. Colorful paints adorned the walls, and shelves were lined with jars of sparkling glitter and stacks of papers filled with sketches and ideas. The characters marveled at the sight, their eyes wide with anticipation.

King Creativity, a wise and gentle ruler, welcomed them with open arms. His eyes twinkled with creativity, and his smile exuded warmth. He understood the power of a supportive environment for nurturing creativity and was eager to share his wisdom with the young dreamers.

"Welcome, my dear friends," King Creativity said, his voice filled with enthusiasm.

"Here in my workshop, we celebrate the magic of imagination and the boundless potential within each of you. Let us embark on a journey of discovery."

King Creativity led the characters through the workshop, showcasing various projects and inventions. They witnessed artists painting vibrant landscapes, musicians composing melodies that stirred the soul, and inventors bringing their ingenious contraptions to life.

As they explored, Luna spoke softly to the characters, emphasizing the importance of a supportive environment for nurturing creativity. She explained that in the workshop, ideas were celebrated, mistakes were seen as opportunities for growth, and collaboration was key. King Creativity encouraged them to trust their instincts, take risks, and embrace the joy of exploration.

After a mesmerizing tour, King Creativity gathered the characters in a circle. With a gleam in his eyes, he announced,

"Today, my young dreamers, I have a special gift for each of you—a creative crown."

He explained that the creative crown symbolized their potential as innovative leaders. When worn, it would serve as a reminder of their unique creative capabilities and the responsibility they held to inspire others.

One by one, King Creativity placed a crown upon the heads of the characters. As the crowns touched their fur, feathers, or scales, a surge of confidence and excitement coursed through them. They felt a deep connection to their creative essence, realizing that within them lay a wellspring of ideas waiting to be released.

With their creative crowns adorning their heads, the characters felt a renewed sense of purpose and possibility. They understood that leadership was not limited to ruling with authority but also encompassed the ability to inspire, innovate, and create positive change.

As they entered the Kingdom of Imagination, the characters were greeted by a fantastical sight. Sparkling crystals hung from branches, casting colorful reflections all around. The air was filled with the scent of blooming flowers, and a gentle breeze carried whispers of inspiration.

Their guide through this enchanting realm was Pixie, a sprightly creature with wings as delicate as butterfly wings. Pixie explained that the kingdom was a haven for creative minds, a place where imagination knew no bounds. She led them to the central courtyard, where a grand gathering was taking place.

Creatives from all corners of the kingdom had assembled, each showcasing their unique talents and ideas. Artists painted murals on towering walls, inventors displayed their imaginative contraptions, and writers recited tales that transported listeners to distant lands. The characters were mesmerized by the kaleidoscope of creativity before them.

Pixie invited the characters to participate in a series of challenges and collaborative activities designed to unlock their creative potential. The first challenge was the Puzzle of Possibilities—a giant puzzle scattered across the courtyard. Working together, the characters pieced together fragments of ideas, realizing that by combining their strengths and perspectives, they could create something truly remarkable.

Next, they ventured into the Gardens of Innovation, where they encountered a maze of riddles and obstacles. Each challenge required them to think creatively, find alternative solutions, and embrace unconventional approaches. They learned that innovation thrived when they embraced curiosity and dared to think outside the box.

The final activity took them to the Hall of Imagination, a chamber filled with whimsical objects and interactive installations. Here, the characters were encouraged to explore their imaginative abilities. They painted murals, sculpted clay into fantastical creatures, and wrote stories that wove together dreams and reality. They realized that their creativity was boundless and that their ideas had the power to shape the world around them.

As they bid farewell to King Creativity and his workshop, the characters carried the spark of creativity within them. They knew that the journey of leadership was intertwined with their creative exploration, and they were determined to nurture their ideas, share their visions, and make a difference in the Enchanted Forest.

Back in the heart of the forest, Luna, Thistle, Buzz, and their friends gathered beneath the moonlit sky. Their creative crowns shimmered in the gentle glow, reminding them of their potential as innovative leaders. They shared their dreams, sketched visions of a brighter future, and pledged to support one another on their creative journeys.

In the weeks and months that followed, the characters embarked on their creative endeavors. Thistle discovered a talent for storytelling, weaving tales that brought joy and inspiration to others. Buzz, with his unwavering determination, created a garden of colorful flowers, attracting bees and butterflies from far and wide. Each character embraced their unique creative gifts, fostering an environment of collaboration and encouragement.

As time passed, the Enchanted Forest bloomed with creativity and innovation. The characters' efforts touched the lives of their fellow creatures, inspiring them to explore their creative potential. The workshop of King Creativity became a symbol of hope, a place where dreams flourished and new ideas took flight.

In the end, the characters realized that their visit to King Creativity's Workshop was not just a one-time experience. It was a facilitator for a lifelong journey of discovery, where they would continue to explore, learn, and create, always guided by the belief that within them, they held the power to shape their world with their unique creative capabilities.

And so, the Enchanted Forest became a point of imagination and innovation, where every creature celebrated their creative crown and embraced the limitless possibilities of their creative leadership.

Lay down your head on your cozy bed
Snuggle up tight, and rest your weary head.
Dreams will come, like stories in your mind
as you drift off to a world so kind.

Chapter 9

Captain Curiosity's Quest

***

In the Enchanted Forest, where whispers of curiosity echoed through the ancient trees, there existed a magical cove known as the Cove of Wonders. This extraordinary place was the dwelling of none other than Captain Curiosity, an adventurous explorer with an insatiable thirst for knowledge.

As the enchanted trio—Luna the Wise Owl, Buzz the Brave Little Bee, and Princess Harmony— ventured deeper into the forest, they heard tales of the wondrous Cove of Curiosity. Legends spoke of a magical haven where books whispered ancient stories, maps unfolded into realms of discovery, and artifacts held the secrets of distant lands.

With hearts brimming with anticipation, Luna, Buzz, and Princess Harmony followed the enchanted trail that led them to the Cove of Wonders. As they approached, the air became tinged with the scent of adventure, and the entrance shimmered with an inviting glow.

Upon entering the cove, the trio found themselves surrounded by towering bookshelves adorned with volumes that seemed to hum with untold tales. Maps adorned the walls, each holding the promise of unexplored territories, and artefacts from far-off places glistened with the allure of mystery.

At the heart of the cove stood Captain Curiosity, a figure draped in a cloak adorned with patches from countless expeditions. The captain's eyes sparkled with the light of inquisitiveness, and an old compass dangled from a leather belt—a testament to the journeys embarked upon.

"Ahoy, fellow seekers of knowledge!" boomed Captain Curiosity, a wide grin revealing the excitement that filled the air.

> *"Welcome to the Cove of Wonders, where every page turned, every map unfolded, and every artefact discovered sparks the flame of curiosity within."*

As Luna, Buzz and Princess Harmony explored the cove, Captain Curiosity shared tales of daring escapades, where the pursuit of knowledge led to the unveiling of hidden wonders. They heard of distant lands explored, mysteries worn, and the joy of discovering the unknown.

The adventurous spirit of Captain Curiosity conveyed a profound lesson—that curiosity and a love for learning were the compasses guiding the way in leadership.

"Leadership," Captain Curiosity emphasized, "is not just about giving commands but about asking questions, exploring the uncharted, and encouraging others to embark on their quests for knowledge."

Inspired by the tales and surrounded by the magic of the cove, Luna, Buzz, and Princess Harmony felt the spark of curiosity igniting within them. Luna envisioned a library where the wisdom of the Enchanted Forest was cataloged, Buzz dreamt of a Garden of Discovery where every flower held a lesson, and Princess Harmony imagined a place where empathy and understanding were the artifacts that shaped the world.

Before parting ways, Captain Curiosity presented them each with a small, ancient-looking key.

"These keys," the captain explained, "unlock the doors to realms undiscovered. May they remind you that the pursuit of knowledge is a lifelong adventure."

As Luna, Buzz, and Princess Harmony left the Cove of Wonders, the enchanted forest echoed with the sound of rustling pages, the distant hum of maps being unfurled, and the soft clinking of keys unlocking doors to new possibilities. The lesson learned from Captain Curiosity lingered in the air—a reminder that curiosity was not just the path to knowledge but the key to unlocking the extraordinary in every corner of the Enchanted Forest.

In their journey through the Cove of Wonders, Luna, Buzz, and Princess Harmony found themselves entangled in the magical threads of challenges, exploration, and the pursuit of knowledge. Captain Curiosity, sensing their eagerness to unravel the mysteries around them, beckoned them to partake in a series of trials that would test their intellect, courage, and unwavering curiosity.

The first challenge took them to the Whispering Archives, a mystical section of the cove where ancient scrolls whispered forgotten tales. Luna, with her wisdom, deciphered cryptic scripts, unveiling the tales of long-lost civilizations. Buzz, the Brave Little Bee, navigated the Buzzing Maze of Conundrums, facing puzzles that required not just bravery but also an inquisitive mind. Princess Harmony, guided by her empathetic heart, delved into the Echoing Cavern of Stories, where the walls resonated with the untold narratives of enchanted beings.

These challenges were not mere obstacles but gateways to a deeper understanding of the joy and value of continuous curiosity. Luna, Buzz, and Princess Harmony discovered that curiosity was not a fleeting moment but an ever-evolving journey—one that required not just answers but an insatiable hunger for more questions.

As they explored new territories within the cove, the trio stumbled upon the Enigma Garden, a place where flowers bloomed with knowledge, each petal a question waiting to be unfolded. Luna, using her wisdom, translated the floral language, revealing the secrets of the interconnected ecosystem. Buzz, with his bravery, faced the Thorny Riddles, extracting wisdom from the prickly challenges. Princess Harmony, with her empathetic touch, conversed with the Blossom of Understanding, where every petal held a story of unity.

Through these explorations, the characters began to appreciate the intricate dance between challenges and the joy derived from unraveling the secrets they held. Captain Curiosity, observing their growth, commended them for embracing the essence of continuous curiosity—the realization that every answer led to new questions, and every challenge was a stepping stone to a broader understanding.

The trio, now adorned with badges of achievement and keys gleaming with newfound wisdom, stood at the heart of the Cove of Wonders. Captain Curiosity, the compass of their journey, imparted a final piece of advice. "Curiosity is a flame that never extinguishes; it only grows brighter with every question asked. May your keys unlock not just doors but endless possibilities as you journey through the realms of continuous curiosity."

With the echoes of Captain Curiosity's wisdom resonating in their hearts, Luna, Buzz, and Princess Harmony left the Cove of Wonders. The enchanted forest, alive with the whispers of their experiences, awaited the next chapter of their never-ending adventure—a journey fueled by the joy and value of continuous curiosity.

Part II:
Games and Activities for Kid Leadership Development

Chapter 10

Leadership Treasure Hunt

In the story of the Enchanted Forest, where ancient trees whispered secrets and colorful flowers bloomed in harmony, Luna the Wise Owl, Buzz the Brave Little Bee, and Princess Harmony found themselves summoned to the Great Oak by the illustrious Enchanted Creatures Council. The council, draped in shimmering robes, announced an unprecedented event – the inaugural Leadership Treasure Hunt.

As beams of golden sunlight danced upon the trio, the Council presented them with ornate scrolls that, when unfurled, transformed into magical maps. Each map pulsated with the promise of adventure, revealing hidden challenges in far corners of the Enchanted Forest. Their quest was to embark on an outdoor odyssey, solving mysteries and unlocking the secrets of leadership.

"Dear Luna, Buzz, and Harmony," intoned the Council,

"The Enchanted Forest beckons you to Wisdom Grove, Teamwork Clearing, Reflection Pool, and the Rainbow Bridge. Embrace the challenges, for they are stepping stones on the path to true leadership."

With a flutter of wings and a buzz of excitement, the trio set forth, the magical map guiding them through sunlit meadows and beneath canopies of ancient oaks. The first challenge awaited them in Wisdom Grove – "Nature Sounds." As they closed their eyes and listened, the forest revealed its symphony. Birds orchestrated a melody, left whispered secrets, and water murmured tales. Luna, Buzz, and Harmony emerged with heightened senses, realizing that leadership involves not only seeing but also listening, attuning themselves to the rhythms of nature.

Journeying deeper into the Enchanted Forest, they arrived at Teamwork Clearing. Here, in the golden embrace of the meadow, challenges unfolded – the Three-Legged Race of Unity and the Balancing Act of Harmony. Laughter echoed as Luna, Buzz, and Harmony discovered the joy of collective effort. Through play, they learned that true leaders foster unity, turning challenges into shared triumphs.

Their map led them to the tranquil Reflection Pool, where still waters held reflections not only of appearance but also of character. Inspired, they replicated the pool at home, filling it with objects symbolizing their essence. Gazing into the water, they grasped the profound lesson that understanding oneself is a cornerstone of effective leadership.

At last, they reached the resplendent Rainbow Bridge, adorned with vibrant hues. Armed with brushes and colours, they engaged in the creation of a "Rainbow Art" project. Each colour represented a unique quality, and as they intertwined their hues, the bridge illustrated the beauty born from celebrating differences.

The grand finale unfolded beneath the wise boughs of the Grand Oak. The Council, assembled in a circle, lauded Luna, Buzz, and Princess Harmony for applying leadership skills with joy. It was a moment to reflect on their journey, a journey that surpassed the physical challenges, marking a symbolic ascent toward leadership greatness.

The Leadership Treasure Hunt had not just been an adventure; it was a chapter of enchantment and growth. Luna, Buzz, and Princess Harmony, as they celebrated amidst the magical glow of the Grand Oak, realized that leadership was not a destination but an ongoing journey, and the Enchanted Forest echoed with laughter – a tribute to the transformative magic of learning and joy in leadership.

In the Enchanted Forest, something exciting was happening! Luna the Wise Owl, Buzz the Brave Little Bee, and Princess Harmony were invited to join the first-ever Leadership Treasure Hunt. The Enchanted Creatures Council, dressed in sparkly robes, told them all about it. But here is your chance to join them on this playful journey where you can get a chance to showcase your creativity with the Enchanted Forest!

Activity 1

Drawing Personal Maps

****

The Council gave each friend a special scroll. Using paper, colours, and stickers, they drew their magical maps with places like Wisdom Grove, Teamwork Clearing, Reflection Pool, and Rainbow Bridge. This was super fun and made the adventure feel like their very own.

"Get ready for a magical adventure, young leaders!" said the Council.

"The Enchanted Forest is full of surprises and challenges. You'll magically learn important leadership skills."

Location 1

Wisdom Grove - Listening to Nature

****

In Wisdom Grove, the friends played a game called "Nature Sounds." They closed their eyes and listened to the forest—birds chirping, leaves rustling, and water flowing. Afterwards, they shared what they heard. It was a cool way to pay attention and enjoy nature.

Location 2

Teamwork Clearing - Fun Challenges

****

The map took them to Teamwork Clearing, a sunny meadow. The friends set up games like the Three-Legged Race of Unity and the Balancing Act of Harmony. They invited others to join, learning that teamwork helps overcome challenges.

"As you explore more, you'll find the Reflection Pool—a special place where the water shows not just how you look but also who you are inside."

Location 3

Reflection Pool - Knowing Yourself

At the Reflection Pool, the friends saw their reflections in the water. They created their own "Reflection Pond" at home with a bowl of water. They put small things inside that represented their qualities. It was a cool way to think about who they are.

Location 4

Rainbow Bridge - Celebrating Differences

****

Next, they reached the Rainbow Bridge. Using different colors, the friends made a "Rainbow Art" project. Each color stood for something special. It showed them that being different is something to celebrate.

Grand Finale

The Grand Oak - Looking Back

****

At the end of the adventure, they arrived at the Grand Oak—a big, wise tree. They gathered to talk about their journey. The Council praised them for using leadership skills with joy. It was a special time to look back and feel proud.

The Leadership Treasure Hunt was not just a story. It was like a magical game that young friends could play, too. As Luna, Buzz, and Princess Harmony celebrated, the Enchanted Forest echoed with laughter—a sign of the magic of learning and joy.

Activity 2

Puzzle Pazoola

****

In Puzzle, Palooza, Luna, Buzz, and Princess Harmony discovered magical jigsaw puzzles scattered across the clearing. Each puzzle piece symbolized a unique leadership quality, such as teamwork, creativity, and resilience. As the characters collaborated to solve the puzzles, they learned that effective leaders bring together different qualities to create a strong and harmonious team. The lesson was clear – just like completing a puzzle, leadership is about combining diverse strengths for success.

Activity 3

Magical Planting

****

At the Enchanted Nursery, characters planted their own "Leadership Seeds" in tiny pots. As they carefully nurtured the seeds, the young adventurers discovered the importance of patience and responsibility in leadership. The lesson learned was that leadership, like growing a plant, requires continuous care, attention, and time. Through this hands-on activity, they understood the value of nurturing their leadership skills over time.

Activity 4

Friendship Bracelet Ceremony

****

In Friendship Grove, characters crafted vibrant friendship bracelets, exchanging them as symbols of their strong connections. This activity emphasized the significance of building strong friendships and supporting one another, teaching the lesson that effective leaders cultivate and cherish meaningful relationships. It highlighted the importance of teamwork, empathy, and collaboration as essential leadership qualities.

Activity 5

Enchanted Dance-Off

****

The Grove of Firefly Lights turned into a dance floor where characters participated in a lively dance-off. Through dance, they expressed themselves freely, discovering that leadership can be joyful and expressive. The lesson here was that effective leaders are not afraid to showcase their creativity and individuality. It encouraged the characters to embrace their unique qualities and express themselves confidently.

Activity 6

Magic Words Wall

****

A mystical wall with blank cards and markers appeared, and characters wrote positive and encouraging words. This interactive activity underscored the impact of uplifting language in leadership. The lesson learned was that effective leaders use positive and encouraging words to create a supportive and motivating environment. It emphasized the power of language in fostering a positive team culture.

Activity 7

Friendship Tree of Trust

****

In a serene grove, characters crafted their "Friendship Tree of Trust," contributing leaves with trust-building activities or promises. This activity reinforced the importance of trust and reliability in leadership. The lesson was that effective leaders prioritize building trust within their team, creating a foundation for open communication and collaboration.

Activity 8

Gratitude Stones

****

At the Gratitude Grove, characters decorated stones with symbols of gratitude. This activity highlighted the importance of recognizing and acknowledging the efforts of others in leadership. The lesson learned was that effective leaders express gratitude, creating a positive and appreciative atmosphere within the team.

Lessons Learned

****

Through the enchanting adventures and interactive activities in the Leadership Treasure Hunt, Luna, Buzz, and Princess Harmony embark on a journey of discovery. Each activity serves as a magical gateway, imparting valuable lessons that lay the foundation for essential leadership skills. As they draw their maps, engage in challenges, and celebrate the uniqueness of each other, young readers will uncover meaningful insights, shaping their understanding of leadership whimsically and memorably. Join the trio on this transformative quest, where the application of each activity has key lessons, fostering a foundation for growth, collaboration, and joyful leadership.

Activity 1

Drawing Personal Maps

Through the creative process of drawing personal maps, Luna, Buzz, and Princess Harmony discovered that leadership is a unique journey, and each individual has their magical path. This activity emphasized the importance of embracing one's individuality and understanding that leadership skills can be expressed in diverse ways.

Location 1

Wisdom Grove - Listening to Nature

In the serene Wisdom Grove, the friends learned that attentive listening is a crucial leadership skill. By tuning in to the sounds of nature, they understood the significance of paying attention to others and their surroundings. This activity instilled the lesson that effective leaders listen actively to gather valuable insights.

Location 2

Teamwork Clearing - Fun Challenges

The Teamwork Clearing activities demonstrated that leadership is not a solo journey but a collective effort. Luna, Buzz, and Princess Harmony discovered that collaboration and teamwork are essential for overcoming challenges. The lesson here was that effective leader's value and encourage the strengths of their team members.

Location 3

Reflection Pool - Knowing Yourself

***

At the Reflection Pool, the friends delved into the importance of self-awareness. Seeing their reflections in the water prompted them to think about their qualities. This activity taught them that effective leaders understand themselves, acknowledging their strengths and areas for growth.

Location 4

Rainbow Bridge - Celebrating Differences

****

The Rainbow Bridge activity conveyed the lesson that effective leaders celebrate diversity. Using different colours to create a symbolic Rainbow Art project emphasized the beauty of differences. It encouraged Luna, Buzz, and Princess Harmony to appreciate and embrace the unique qualities of themselves and others.

Grand Finale

The Grand Oak - Looking Back

****

Lesson Learned: The Grand Oak gathering served as a reflective space, emphasizing the importance of looking back on the leadership journey. The friends learned that effective leaders take the time to reflect on their experiences, celebrate achievements, and identify areas for further growth. It instilled a sense of pride and accomplishment.

Activity 2

Puzzle Palooza

****

Puzzle Palooza taught Luna, Buzz, and Princess Harmony that effective leaders are like skilled puzzle solvers. The activity emphasized the value of combining various leadership qualities, just as different puzzle pieces come together to form a complete picture. It highlighted that diversity in leadership strengths contributes to overall success.

Activity 3

Magical Planting

The Magical Planting activity instilled the lesson that leadership, like nurturing a plant, requires patience and consistent care. Luna, Buzz, and Princess Harmony learned that effective leaders invest time and attention in developing their skills, allowing them to grow and flourish over time.

Activity 4

Friendship Bracelet Ceremony

Crafting friendship bracelets in Friendship Grove emphasized the importance of meaningful connections in leadership. The lesson was that effective leaders prioritize building strong relationships and fostering an environment of trust, collaboration, and empathy within their team.

Activity 5

Enchanted Dance-Off

The Enchanted Dance-Off conveyed that leadership can be expressed joyfully and creatively. Luna, Buzz, and Princess Harmony discovered that effective leaders embrace their unique qualities, expressing themselves confidently. It highlighted the idea that joy and self-expression are essential aspects of leadership.

Activity 6

Magic Words Wall

The Magic Words Wall activity underscored the impact of positive language in leadership. The lesson was that effective leaders use uplifting words to create a supportive and motivating environment. It emphasized the power of language in shaping a positive team culture.

Activity 7

Friendship Tree of Trust

Crafting the Friendship Tree of Trust in a serene grove reinforced the importance of trust and reliability in leadership. Luna, Buzz, and Princess Harmony learned that effective leaders prioritize building trust within their team, creating a foundation for open communication and collaboration.

Activity 8

Gratitude Stones

Decorating Gratitude Stones in the Gratitude Grove highlighted the significance of expressing gratitude in leadership. The activity conveyed that effective leaders recognize and appreciate the efforts of others, fostering a positive and appreciative atmosphere within the team.

Chapter 11

Storyboard Leadership
***

Luna the Wise Owl, Buzz the Brave Little Bee, and Princess Harmony stumbled upon an extraordinary glade bathed in the soft glow of twilight. In the centre stood the Celestial Sapling, a magnificent tree that radiated wisdom and serenity, symbolizing personal and leadership growth.

As Luna, Buzz, and Princess Harmony marvelled at the Celestial Sapling, the air resonated with a melodious hum, and the wise owl, perceiving the mystical aura, uttered,

"Behold, dear travellers, the Celestial Sapling, a beacon of growth and leadership. Your tales shall be inscribed upon its leaves, and in return, it shall impart its enchantment upon your journey."

The Celestial Sapling, recognizing the trio's potential, bestowed upon them enchanted sketchbooks. Luna's sketchbook shimmered with celestial patterns, Buzz's with the vibrancy of blooming flowers, and Princess Harmony's with the hues of a harmonious melody.

Luna, with her keen wisdom, sketched the stories of her decisions and their profound impacts. The Celestial Sapling responded by unfurling leaves that sparkled with the discernment gained from Luna's experiences.

Buzz, the valiant bee with a heart full of courage, chronicled tales of daring escapades and encounters with challenges. The Celestial Sapling adorned itself with leaves that gleamed with the resilience and bravery demonstrated by Buzz.

Princess Harmony, representing harmony in diversity, painted her sketchbook with stories of unity and collaboration among the Enchanted Creatures. The Celestial Sapling swayed in rhythmic acknowledgement, leaves reflecting the vibrancy of the Princess's commitment to harmony.

As Luna, Buzz, and Princess Harmony continued to sketch, the Celestial Sapling began to grow in tandem with their narratives. Its trunk absorbed the essence of their wisdom, courage, and harmony, and its branches intertwined like a tapestry of shared leadership.

In a moment of synchronicity, the Celestial Sapling's leaves emitted a harmonious melody, echoing the interconnectedness of personal and leadership growth. Luna, Buzz, and Princess Harmony felt a profound connection to the magical tree, recognizing that their journey was now intricately woven into the fabric of the Enchanted Forest.

With a final stroke of their enchanted sketchbooks, Luna, Buzz, and Princess Harmony acknowledged the reciprocal relationship between personal and leadership growth. The Celestial Sapling, now resplendent with their stories, stood as a testament to the power of shared experiences and the transformative nature of leadership.

As the trio bid farewell to the Celestial Sapling, they carried not just sketchbooks filled with tales but a deep understanding that leadership, like the Celestial Sapling, flourishes in the soil of collaboration and shared narratives. The Enchanted Forest echoed with the harmonious song of growth, as Luna, Buzz, and Princess Harmony ventured forth, their leadership intertwined with the mystical energy of the Celestial Sapling. But here is your chance to join them on this playful journey where you can get a chance to showcase your creativity with the Enchanted Forest!

Activity 1

Enchanted Tree Growth Chart

Begin by creating a large Enchanted Tree Growth Chart on a wall or poster board. Outline a magical tree with branches and roots. Provide children with colorful paper leaves and markers. Each child can write their name on a leaf and draw a symbol or picture representing a personal or leadership goal. As they achieve these goals, they can add more leaves to their branches, visually tracking their progress over time.

Activity 2

Storytelling Sketchbooks

Distribute blank sketchbooks and a variety of art supplies. Encourage children to personalize their Storytelling Sketchbooks by decorating the covers with magical themes. Instruct them to draw and narrate their leadership stories within the pages. Emphasize the inclusion of imaginative elements and characters. Create a storytelling circle where each child can share excerpts from their sketchbooks.

Activity 3

Leaf Rubbing Leadership Collage

Collect a variety of leaves from different plants. Provide each child with paper and crayons. Instruct them to place the leaves under the paper and gently rub over them with crayons to create leaf rubbings. Once completed, encourage the children to arrange their rubbings into a Leadership Collage. They can add symbols or words that represent qualities they admire in leaders.

Activity 4

Friendship Tree Ceremony

Set up a Friendship Tree using a small potted plant or a crafted tree structure. During a special ceremony, provide children with colorful ribbons or strings. Ask them to tie a ribbon onto the tree, each representing a positive action or quality related to leadership and friendship. Encourage a discussion where each child explains the significance of their ribbon.

Activity 5

Leadership Crown Crafting

Supply materials such as colourful paper, stickers, markers, and glitter for Leadership Crown Crafting. Guide children in designing their own crowns, encouraging them to include symbols or words that represent their leadership qualities. After completing the crowns, initiate a celebratory ceremony where each child wears their creation proudly.

Activity 6

Magic Wand Creations

Organize a Magic Wand Crafting session with materials such as cardboard, glitter, ribbons, and markers. Guide children in designing their own personalized magic wands. Encourage them to incorporate symbols or colors representing their leadership strengths and aspirations. After completing their wands, allow them to share the significance of their design choices with the group.

Lessons Learned

***

Activity 1

Enchanted Tree Growth Chart

This activity deeply instils the concept of growth and progress. Children learn the value of setting and achieving goals, understanding that effort and perseverance lead to positive outcomes. The visual representation of their accomplishments on the tree reinforces the joy of personal and leadership development. This activity teaches children the importance of setting and achieving personal and leadership goals over time. By visually tracking their progress on the magical tree, children learn the value of perseverance and the satisfaction that comes with accomplishing objectives. Each leaf on the tree becomes a symbol of their individual growth, fostering a sense of responsibility and self-motivation. This activity encourages children to reflect on their journey, instilling the lesson that consistent effort and goal-setting are vital components of personal and leadership development.

Activity 2

Storytelling Sketchbooks

This activity enhances creativity and storytelling skills. Children express their thoughts and experiences through both visual and written mediums, fostering effective communication. The uniqueness of each child's sketchbook reinforces the idea that everyone's leadership journey is special and individual. Children get into the kingdom of creativity and self-expression, discovering the power of narrating their leadership stories. Personalizing sketchbooks with magical themes fosters a sense of ownership and pride in their narratives. Sharing excerpts within a storytelling circle promotes effective communication, and the imaginative elements allow children to explore diverse perspectives. The lesson learned is that storytelling is a dynamic tool for self-discovery and sharing experiences, cultivating a rich understanding of leadership through the lens of personal narratives.

Activity 3

Leaf Rubbing Leadership Collage

The Leaf Rubbing Leadership Collage encourages children to appreciate diversity and recognize admirable leadership qualities. Through this artistic expression, they understand the beauty in embracing various attributes, both in themselves and others. It encourages children to appreciate and emulate leadership qualities through a tactile and visual experience. Creating leaf rubbings requires careful observation and patience, instilling qualities like attention to detail and perseverance. Arranging these rubbings into a Leadership Collage promotes the exploration of admired leadership qualities. By symbolically connecting leaves to leadership traits, children learn to identify and appreciate positive attributes in themselves and others, fostering a sense of admiration for diverse leadership qualities.

Activity 4

Friendship Tree Ceremony

This activity emphasizes the importance of positive actions and qualities in leadership. Children understand that collectively contributing positive elements leads to the growth of a harmonious community, symbolized by the Friendship Tree. This activity instils the significance of positive actions and qualities related to leadership and friendship. Tying ribbons onto the Friendship Tree becomes a tangible representation of collective values, creating a shared visual symbol of unity. Discussing the ribbons encourages open communication, teaching children to express the meaning behind their actions. The lesson learned is that leadership is intertwined with positive actions and shared values, emphasizing the importance of fostering a supportive and inclusive community.

Activity 5

Leadership Crown Crafting

Crafting Leadership Crowns promotes a sense of empowerment and pride in one's leadership abilities. Through this hands-on activity, children learn to embrace and celebrate their unique strengths, fostering confidence and positive self-perception within the group. It empowers children to express their leadership qualities creatively. Designing crowns with symbols and words reinforces the idea that leadership can be a source of pride. The celebratory ceremony where children proudly wear their crowns emphasizes the significance of recognizing and celebrating one's leadership strengths. This activity teaches children that leadership is something to be embraced and showcased with confidence, fostering a positive and empowered mindset.

Activity 6

Magic Wand Creations

Crafting magic wands promotes creative expression and individuality. Children learn that their unique qualities, like the features on their wands, are sources of strength in their leadership journey. This hands-on activity provides a tangible reminder of their abilities to make positive impacts. This activity introduces the concept of leadership as a magical and empowering force. Crafting personalized wands allows children to visually represent their unique leadership strengths and aspirations. Sharing the significance of their designs promotes self-reflection and effective communication. The lesson learned is that leadership is a transformative and individualized journey, and each child possesses the magic within themselves to make a positive impact. This activity encourages a sense of empowerment and self-belief in their leadership abilities.

Chapter **12**

Building a Kindness Kingdom

In the kingdom of Enchanted Forest, Enchanted Grove, where sunbeams filtered through the ancient branches of the Great Oak, Luna the Wise Owl, Buzz the Brave Little Bee, and Princess Harmony gathered in the soft glow of twilight. The air buzzed with anticipation, for the Enchanted Creatures Council, adorned in shimmering robes, had revealed the quest for a most extraordinary creation—a magical tree sculpture that would symbolize the growth of friendship and kindness in their shared forest kingdom.

The Council bestowed upon Luna, Buzz, and Princess Harmony a treasure trove of materials—feathers from the wisest owls, honey-infused golden nectar, vines that hummed with harmony, and leaves that shimmered like dew-kissed rainbows. Each component held the essence of enchantment, awaiting the touch of the characters to weave them into a living masterpiece.

Finding a secluded grove beneath the Great Oak's sprawling branches, the trio embarked on their artistic journey. Luna's wings moved with the precision of a master sculptor, shaping the trunk and branches with the grace born of centuries of wisdom. Buzz darted through the air, adding golden droplets of nectar that sparkled like morning sunlight. Princess Harmony, with a gentle touch, intertwined the vines, infusing the sculpture with the very melodies that echoed in her heart.

As the magical tree took form, the Enchanted Creatures Council presented a collection of leaves and ornaments; each imbued with the potential to capture acts of kindness. Luna delicately inscribed her leaf with profound words of wisdom shared with fellow creatures. Buzz crafted an ornament that glimmered with tales of bravery and resilience. Princess Harmony's leaf bore the hues of shared melodies and the beauty of collaboration.

The characters meticulously connected each leaf or ornament to the Kindness Tree, ensuring that every piece found its place in the narrative of shared benevolence. A symphony of laughter and the gentle rustle of leaves accompanied the crafting process, echoing through the enchanted grove.

The arts and crafts session transformed into a transcendent experience, transcending the boundaries of mere creation. It became a medium for expressing and reinforcing positive values, with Luna, Buzz, and Princess Harmony pouring their individuality and spirit into each piece. The Kindness Tree, now adorned with a kaleidoscope of leaves, emanated an energy that reverberated with the essence of their collective goodwill.

The magical and enchanting elements of the project seamlessly wove into a tapestry of whimsical narrative. Luna, Buzz, and Princess Harmony, pausing to admire their creation, felt the collective warmth of their shared kindness. The Kindness Tree stood not just as a sculpture but as a living testament to the transformative power of friendship, kindness, and collaborative endeavours.

The Enchanted Creatures Council, witnessing the completion of this extraordinary creation, showered Luna, Buzz, and Princess Harmony with praise for their heartfelt contributions. The Kindness Tree, bathed in the soft glow of twilight, became a beacon in the Enchanted Grove, radiating a gentle glow that beckoned others to embrace the magic of kindness.

As the characters revelled in the joy of creating something beautiful together, the Great Oak itself seemed to murmur in approval. The story of Luna, Buzz, and Princess Harmony and their Kindness Tree echoed through the Enchanted Forest, inspiring readers to embark on their quests of collaborative kindness. The Enchanted Grove, forever touched by the enchantment of friendship and kindness, whispered the tale to those who ventured beneath its ancient branches, carrying the magic of the Kindness Tree in their hearts. But here is your chance to join them on this playful journey where you can get a chance to showcase your creativity with the Enchanted Forest!

Activity 1

Kindness Tree Creation Friendship and Positive Values

A heartwarming journey with the creation of a magical Kindness Tree, symbolizing the blossoming of friendship and kindness in the Enchanted Forest. This activity not only allows young readers to engage in arts and crafts but also encourages them to embody positive values through a collaborative project.

Gathering Supplies: Gather art supplies such as colorful paper, scissors, glue, and markers. Ensure a variety of materials to add a magical touch to the tree, like glitter, sequins, or beads.

Introduction to the Kindness Tree: Begin by introducing the concept of the Kindness Tree within the Enchanted Forest. Explain that each leaf or ornament on the tree will represent an act of kindness contributed by a character.

Character Connection: Have each child or group of children choose an Enchanted Forest character. Encourage them to think about the unique qualities of their character and how they can translate these qualities into acts of kindness.

Creation of Leaves/Ornaments: Using the selected art supplies, guide the children in crafting leaves or ornaments that represent acts of kindness. Each creation should showcase the character's unique contribution to fostering friendship and positivity.

Connecting to the Magical Tree: As the leaves or ornaments are completed, guide the children in attaching them to the branches of a central tree sculpture. This collaborative effort symbolizes the collective growth of friendship and kindness within the Enchanted Forest.

Reflective Discussion: After completing the Kindness Tree, facilitate a discussion about the acts of kindness depicted on each leaf or ornament. Encourage the children to share their thoughts on how small gestures contribute to a positive and harmonious environment.

Interactive Storytelling: Transform the activity into an interactive storytelling session. As each leaf or ornament is placed on the tree, weave a whimsical narrative around the Enchanted Forest characters and their journey toward creating a forest filled with kindness.

Inspiration for Readers: Conclude the activity by expressing how the magical and enchanting elements of the Kindness Tree contribute to a captivating narrative. Encourage young readers to be inspired by the collaborative efforts of the characters and incorporate kindness into their own lives.

Activity 2

Potion Creation Challenge - Teamwork and Innovation

Dive into the magical world of potion-making, where characters work together to create enchanting mixtures. This activity emphasizes teamwork, creativity, and problem-solving.

Gather Ingredients: Provide a variety of safe, non-toxic materials that represent magical ingredients (coloured water, glitter, beads, etc.).

Team Formation: Divide children into small teams. Each team represents a group of characters within the Enchanted Forest.

Potion Creation: Instruct teams to collaborate and create their magical potion using the provided ingredients. Encourage imaginative names and purposes for their concoctions.

Presentation: Each team presents its potion to the group, explaining its magical properties and the teamwork involved in its creation.

Shared Potion Pool: Combine a small amount from each team's potion to create a shared "Enchanted Forest Potion." This symbolizes the collective strength and diversity of the Enchanted Forest.

Activity 3

Enchanted Forest Animal Charades - Communication and Empathy

Bring the Enchanted Forest creatures to life through a game of charades. This activity enhances communication skills and encourages empathy.

Creature Assignments: Assign each child a different Enchanted Forest creature (owl, bee, rabbit, etc.).

Character Immersion: Instruct children to research and embody the characteristics of their assigned creature. Discuss how each creature contributes to the forest ecosystem.

Charades Game: Organize a charades game where children take turns acting out their Enchanted Forest creature without speaking.

Guessing and Discussion: After each charade, encourage others to guess the creature and discuss its role in the forest. This promotes understanding and empathy for different perspectives.

Reflective Circle: Conclude the activity with a reflective circle, where children share their experiences portraying their creatures and the importance of communication in understanding one another.

Activity 4

Rainbow Bridge of Harmony - Unity in Diversity

Explore the concept of unity in diversity through a collaborative art project, the Rainbow Bridge of Harmony.

Colour Representation: Assign each colour of the rainbow a positive quality (red for courage, yellow for kindness, etc.).

Collaborative Art: Provide materials for children to create individual artwork representing their assigned color and quality.

Bridge Construction: Collaboratively arrange the individual artworks to form a vibrant Rainbow Bridge of Harmony. Discuss how the unity of diverse colors creates a beautiful whole.

Symbolic Discussion: Facilitate a discussion on the significance of each color and how it contributes to the overall beauty and strength of the bridge.

Enchanted Bridge Display: Showcase the Rainbow Bridge in a central location within the Enchanted Forest, symbolizing the unity achieved through embracing diversity.

Activity 5

Enchanted Forest Story Stones - Creativity and Collaboration

Spark imagination and collaboration through the creation of Enchanted Forest Story Stones, allowing children to collaboratively construct magical tales.

Gather Stones: Collect smooth stones from the forest, ensuring they are suitable for drawing or painting.

Character Creation: Assign each child or group a specific Enchanted Forest character or element to illustrate on their stone.

Story Circle: Arrange the stones in a circle. Each child or group contributes a part of the story by selecting a stone and incorporating its character or element into the narrative.

Continuation Game: Encourage children to take turns adding to the story by selecting stones and creatively weaving them into the ongoing narrative.

Final Tale: Conclude the activity with a shared storytelling session, showcasing the collaborative tale crafted through the Enchanted Forest Story Stones.

Lessons Learned

***

Activity 1

Kindness Tree Creation

Through the Kindness Tree Creation, children learn that small acts of kindness, when combined, contribute to a positive and harmonious community, emphasizing the value of teamwork and collective effort. Gathering supplies together fosters a sense of unity and cooperation as each child plays a role in preparing for the collaborative project. Introducing the concept of the Kindness Tree emphasizes the importance of fostering positive values within a community, setting the stage for the upcoming creative endeavor. By choosing Enchanted Forest characters and translating their qualities into acts of kindness, children develop empathy and recognize the diverse ways kindness can be expressed. Crafting leaves or ornaments becomes a creative expression of these acts, reinforcing the idea that everyone's contribution, no matter how small, adds to the overall beauty of the community. Attaching leaves to the tree symbolizes teamwork, teaching children that collaboration results in a more significant impact, as seen in the collective growth of the Kindness Tree.

Reflective discussions about the acts of kindness depicted on each leaf or ornament encourage thoughtful reflection, helping children understand the importance of small gestures in creating a positive and harmonious environment. Transforming the activity into an interactive storytelling session weaves a whimsical narrative around the Enchanted Forest characters, inspiring children to see the transformative power of kindness. Concluding with an emphasis on the magical and enchanting elements of the Kindness Tree inspires children to incorporate kindness into their own lives, understanding its ability to create a captivating narrative and a harmonious community.

Activity 2

Potion Creation Challenge - Teamwork and Innovation

Through the Potion Creation Challenge, children learn that effective teamwork involves valuing diverse perspectives and combining strengths to achieve a common goal, fostering innovation and unity. Gathering ingredients becomes a collaborative effort, teaching children that each team member's contribution is vital to the overall success of the potion. Team formation introduces the importance of collaboration, helping children discover that each team member brings a unique perspective and fostering a sense of diversity.

Collaborative potion-making encourages creativity and imaginative thinking, guiding children to combine different ideas to achieve a common goal. Presenting their potions enhances communication skills, as children articulate their thoughts and actively listen to team members. The shared potion pool symbolizes unity and diversity, helping children understand that combining diverse strengths leads to a more potent and harmonious result. Overall, the Potion Creation Challenge instills the lesson that effective teamwork involves valuing diversity, fostering innovation, and achieving unity through collective strength.

Activity 3

Enchanted Forest Animal Charades - Communication and Empathy

Through Enchanted Forest Animal Charades, children learn the importance of effective communication, understanding different perspectives, and embracing diversity within a community. Assigning creatures promotes research and understanding, allowing children to immerse themselves in the characteristics of their assigned creature and fostering empathy. Character immersion deepens the connection to the Enchanted Forest, helping children appreciate the diverse roles each creature plays in the ecosystem.

The charades game hones communication skills, teaching children to convey ideas and emotions through non-verbal cues. Guessing creatures and discussing their roles promote empathy as children gain an understanding of different perspectives and the importance of effective communication. Concluding with a reflective circle encourages open discussion, fostering a sense of community and understanding. Overall, Enchanted Forest Animal Charades instills the lesson that effective communication and empathy are essential for building a harmonious community that embraces diversity.

Activity 4

Rainbow Bridge of Harmony - Unity in Diversity

Through the Rainbow Bridge of Harmony, children discover that unity in diversity creates a stronger and more beautiful community, emphasizing the value of collaboration and appreciation for differences. Assigning positive qualities to colors introduces the concept of diversity, fostering an appreciation for differences among children. Collaborative art creation represents personal contributions, helping children understand that their unique qualities contribute to the overall beauty of the collaborative project. Collaboratively arranging the individual artworks reinforces the idea of unity, as children witness how combining diverse elements results in a beautiful and harmonious whole.

Discussing the significance of each color deepens understanding as children learn that embracing diversity leads to strength and beauty within a community. Showcasing the Rainbow Bridge emphasizes the unity achieved through collaboration, fostering a sense of community accomplishment. Overall, the Rainbow Bridge of Harmony instills the lesson that unity in diversity creates a stronger and more beautiful community, promoting collaboration and an appreciation for differences.

Activity 5

Enchanted Forest Story Stones - Creativity and Collaboration

Through Enchanted Forest Story Stones, children learn the value of creativity and collaboration in constructing engaging narratives, fostering a sense of community storytelling and appreciation for diverse perspectives. Collecting stones for drawing encourages exploration, connecting children with nature while selecting suitable canvases for their creative expressions. Assigning characters or elements encourages individual creativity, allowing children to express their unique perspectives and contribute to the diversity of the collective narrative.

Arranging stones in a circle establishes a sense of community as children take turns contributing to the story, fostering collaborative storytelling skills. Adding to the story through stones promotes creativity and imagination as children build upon each other's ideas, creating a rich and collaborative narrative. Concluding with a shared storytelling session celebrates collaboration, allowing children to witness the imaginative tale crafted through their combined efforts. Overall, Enchanted Forest Story Stones instills the lesson that creativity and collaboration are essential for constructing engaging narratives and fostering a sense of community storytelling, encouraging an appreciation for diverse perspectives.

Hush now, little one, in the pale moon's gleam.
Drift into dreams like a gentle stream.
Moonlight's cradling, a soft melody.
Sweet dreams, little one, in the night's mystery

Chapter **13**

Superhero Leadership Capes
****

The Enchanted Forest where the Forest team gathered with the imagination Springs, where creativity flowed like a magical river, Luna the Wise Owl, Buzz the Brave Little Bee, and Princess Harmony found themselves summoned by the Whimsical Council. The Council, donned in shimmering robes, revealed a quest that transcended the ordinary—an alliance forged through the creation of superhero capes that would symbolize not only their leadership but also their commitment to inspiring positive change.

As the sun dipped below the horizon, casting hues of orange and purple across the sky, Luna, Buzz, and Princess Harmony gathered in the heart of Imagination Springs. The Whimsical Council presented them with a treasure trove of materials—fabric spun from threads of creativity, colours that mirrored the spectrum of virtues, and enchanted emblems that sparkled with the promise of greatness.

In unison, the characters recited a superhero alliance oath, their voices harmonizing with the melodies of the enchanted breeze.

"We pledge to use our leadership capes for the greater good, to soar above challenges, and to inspire positive change in the tapestry of Imagination Springs," they proclaimed, sealing their commitment with a shared vision of a brighter, more harmonious realm.

The act of crafting unfolded into a magical and empowering experience. Luna, with the wisdom of ages, guided the selection of colours that resonated with the essence of leadership. Buzz, with boundless energy, darted from hue to hue, infusing each thread with the bravery that stirred within. Princess Harmony, with a gentle touch, embroidered symbols of unity and collaboration, weaving them seamlessly into the fabric.

As the capes took shape, Luna, Buzz, and Princess Harmony felt the transformative power of their creative endeavour. The capes became more than mere garments; they became extensions of their leadership strengths, shimmering with the virtues that defined their characters. Luna's cape bore the hues of moonlit wisdom, Buzz's cape glowed with the brilliance of bravery, and Princess Harmony's cape flowed with the harmony of shared melodies.

The symbolism of the capes reached beyond their physical form. Each emblem, stitch, and colour became a testament to the characters' commitment to embodying their chosen leadership qualities. Luna's cape whispered sagas of timeless wisdom, Buzz's cape hummed with tales of audacious feats, and Princess Harmony's cape resonated with harmonies that echoed through the realm.

In the final moments of crafting, Luna, Buzz, and Princess Harmony, adorned in their splendid capes, stood before the Whimsical Council. The capes, now infused with the characters' leadership magic, radiated a gentle glow that mirrored the moonlit night. The Whimsical Council, in awe of the transformative journey, applauded their efforts and celebrated the birth of a new alliance.

The collaborative elements of this extraordinary quest left an indelible mark on Imagination Springs. Luna, Buzz, and Princess Harmony, embracing their leadership capes, soared into the night sky, leaving trails of inspiration that danced with the stars. Their journey became a narrative that encouraged readers to explore and celebrate their leadership qualities creatively and imaginatively.

As Luna, Buzz, and Princess Harmony soared across the enchanted sky, their capes billowing in the breeze, a symphony of whispers echoed through Imagination Springs. The realm, forever touched by the magic of collaboration and leadership, embraced the readers in a warm embrace, inviting them to embark on their quests of self-discovery and creativity. The leadership capes, now woven into the very fabric of Imagination Springs, stood as a witness to the transformative power of collaboration and the celebration of unique leadership strengths. But here is your chance to join them on this playful journey where you can get a chance to showcase your creativity with the Enchanted Forest!

Activity 1

Design Your Leadership Cape

For this imaginative crafting adventure, gather essential art supplies such as colourful paper, markers, stickers, fabric scraps, glue, and safety scissors. Begin by inviting young readers to brainstorm and identify their unique leadership qualities. Encourage them to translate these qualities into visual elements while designing their leadership capes. Whether it's using bold colors for courage, adding symbols for creativity, or incorporating patterns for teamwork, this hands-on activity provides a platform for creative expression. Children can cut and glue the materials onto their capes, turning the crafting process into a magical and empowering experience.

Activity 2

Superhero Alliance Oath Ceremony

Transform the act of reciting the superhero alliance oath into an engaging and memorable event. Set the stage with a designated area for the ceremony, perhaps adorned with simple props like a superhero emblem or a "Leadership Torch." Each child, as a superhero, takes turns reciting the oath, pledging to use their leadership capes for positive change. This interactive ceremony not only reinforces their commitment to embodying leadership qualities but also adds an element of playfulness and friendship.

Activity 3

Storytelling with Leadership Capes

Incorporate the leadership capes into a captivating storytelling session. Provide a comfortable storytelling circle where readers can share short stories or scenarios featuring their superhero personas and their leadership adventures. Encourage them to use their capes as storytelling props, enhancing the imaginative experience. This activity not only develops their storytelling and public speaking skills but also reinforces the idea that leadership is an exciting and dynamic journey.

Activity 4

Leadership Cape Parade

Organize a lively "Leadership Cape Parade" to celebrate the creative efforts of the young leaders. Set up a designated parade route, either indoors or in a safe outdoor space. Each child, wearing their leadership cape, walks the parade route while explaining the symbolism behind their design. This public showcase promotes self-confidence, encourages peer support, and reinforces the notion that leadership qualities are unique and worthy of celebration.

Activity 5

Leadership Strengths Showcase

Create a special area, whether physical or virtual, where readers can display their leadership capes along with short descriptions of the strengths and qualities they represent. This showcase provides an opportunity for children to explore and appreciate each other's creations, fostering a sense of community and mutual respect for diverse leadership qualities. Encourage a collaborative discussion about the collective strength that emerges when various leadership qualities come together.

Lessons Learned

Activity 1

Design Your Leadership Cape

In crafting their leadership capes, young readers embark on a journey of self-discovery and creative expression. The lesson learned from this activity is that leadership qualities are unique and personal, and each child has the power to visually represent their strengths through art. The process encourages them to embrace their individuality and recognize the diverse attributes that contribute to effective leadership.

Activity 2

Superhero Alliance Oath Ceremony

Reciting the superhero alliance oath transforms a simple act into a meaningful commitment to positive change. The lesson learned is about the importance of making promises and pledges to embody leadership qualities actively. The ceremony fosters a sense of responsibility and unity among the young readers, emphasizing that leadership is not only about personal growth but also about collective empowerment.

Activity 3

Storytelling with Leadership Capes

Through storytelling with their leadership capes, children learn the art of narrative expression and imaginative communication. The lesson here is that leadership is a dynamic and exciting journey filled with adventures. By sharing their stories, young readers discover the power of using their voices to inspire others and communicate their leadership experiences in a fun and engaging way.

Activity 4

Leadership Cape Parade

The Leadership Cape Parade serves as a celebration of individuality and collective creativity. The lesson learned is that showcasing one's unique leadership qualities can be a joyous and empowering experience. The parade fosters self-confidence and pride in one's abilities while also promoting mutual support and appreciation among the young leaders as they celebrate each other's distinctive capes.

Activity 5

Leadership Strengths Showcase

Creating a showcase for the leadership capes reinforces the idea that diversity in leadership strengths is something to be celebrated and appreciated. The lesson learned is that when different qualities come together, they create a collective strength that enhances the overall community. This activity encourages young readers to recognize and respect the varied leadership attributes in their peers, fostering a sense of unity and understanding.

Chapter **14**

Leader's Puzzle Palace

Deep within the heart of the Enchanted Forest, Luna the Wise Owl, Buzz the Brave Little Bee, and Princess Harmony discovered a mysterious chamber hidden behind a veil of shimmering vines. Intrigued by the unknown, they ventured inside, only to find themselves surrounded by an otherworldly glow that emanated from the walls adorned with enigmatic symbols.

As Luna, Buzz, and Princess Harmony moved further into the chamber, the air crackled with an intellectual challenge.

A holographic image materialized before them, presenting the first riddle:

"I can be cracked, made, told, and played. What am I?"

The riddle echoed through the chamber, demanding not just an answer but a demonstration of their collective intelligence.

Luna, with her vast wisdom, furrowed her feathery brow in thought. Buzz, fueled by bravery, buzzed around, observing the surroundings, while Princess Harmony, with her regal grace, pondered the riddle's nuances. Together, they pieced together the clues and, with a harmonious unity of minds, declared,

"A Joke!"

The chamber resonated with approval as the holographic image dissolved, revealing the next challenge.

The second riddle emerged, etched into the chamber floor:

"The more you take, the more you leave behind. What am I?"

Luna, Buzz, and Princess Harmony engaged in a collaborative discussion, their diverse perspectives weaving a thought bubble. Luna's wisdom recognized the patterns, Buzz's bravery approached the problem with enthusiasm, and Princess Harmony's intuition guided them toward the answer.

"Footsteps!" they exclaimed, and once again, the chamber responded with a radiant glow.

However, the challenges persisted, each riddle more intricate than the last. Luna, Buzz, and Princess Harmony navigated through queries that tested their critical thinking, lateral reasoning, and deductive skills. As they delved deeper, the collaborative synergy of their minds became a beacon of intelligence, lighting up the chamber with their shared brilliance.

The final riddle loomed large, shimmering in golden letters:

"I speak without a mouth and hear without ears. I have no body, but I come alive with the wind. What am I?"

Luna's eyes gleamed with recognition, Buzz's wings fluttered with excitement, and Princess Harmony's regal composure held the answer.

"An Echo!" they declared in unison, and the chamber erupted in a dazzling display of lights.

With the last riddle unravelled, the chamber acknowledged their triumph. As Luna, Buzz, and Princess Harmony stepped out, the Enchanted Forest resonated with the tales of their collaborative intelligence. The winds carried whispers of their journey, inspiring others to seek knowledge, unity, and the boundless magic that lay within the shared brilliance of the Enchanted Trio.

And so, Luna, Buzz, and Princess Harmony continued their adventures, their bond stronger, and their minds forever attuned to the melody of collaborative intelligence that echoed through the Enchanted

Forest. But here is your chance to join them on this playful journey where you can get a chance to showcase your creativity with the Enchanted Forest!

Activity 1

Enchanted Riddle Quest

Invite readers to take on their own Enchanted Riddle Quest. Create a series of riddles that challenge critical thinking and problem-solving skills. Encourage readers to collaborate with friends or family members to unravel the mysteries, fostering teamwork and shared intelligence. Consider incorporating a magical setting or theme to enhance the adventure.

Activity 2

Collaborative Puzzle Creation

Encourage readers to design their collaborative puzzles. This activity promotes creativity and critical thinking as they craft riddles, anagrams, or crossword puzzles. Readers can share their puzzles with friends or family, challenging others to solve the mysteries they've created.

Activity 3

Storytelling through Riddles

Inspire readers to weave riddles into their stories. Encourage them to incorporate riddles that characters must solve as part of the narrative. This activity enhances both storytelling and problem-solving skills, allowing readers to explore the synergy of creativity and critical thinking.

Activity 4

Mindful Meditation and Reflection

Guide readers through a mindful meditation session focused on clearing the mind and enhancing concentration. After the meditation, encourage them to reflect on how moments of clarity and focus can contribute to effective problem-solving, drawing parallels to Luna, Buzz, and Princess Harmony's collaborative intelligence.

Activity 5

Collaborative Art Project

Facilitate a collaborative art project where readers work together to create a visual representation of the Enchanted Riddle Quest. Provide art supplies and encourage them to illustrate scenes from the story, showcasing Luna, Buzz, and Princess Harmony using their collective intelligence to solve riddles. This activity fosters creativity, teamwork, and artistic expression.

Activity 6

Enchanted Forest Exploration

Encourage readers to explore nature in their local environment, akin to Luna, Buzz, and Princess Harmony's adventure in the Enchanted Forest. This outdoor activity promotes observation, curiosity, and an appreciation for the natural world, fostering a sense of connection to the magical elements found in the story.

Activity 7

Virtual Escape Room Challenge

Organize a virtual escape room challenge for readers. Create an online experience with riddles and puzzles that participants must solve collaboratively. This activity not only enhances critical thinking skills but also provides an interactive and engaging way for readers to experience the thrill of problem-solving.

Lessons Learned
****

Activity 1

Enchanted Riddle Quest

Readers discover the power of collaboration and critical thinking. Engaging in the Enchanted Riddle Quest, Luna, Buzz, and Princess Harmony realize that combining their unique strengths and perspectives leads to solving complex challenges. This activity emphasizes that teamwork is not only about sharing ideas but also valuing diverse contributions, showcasing that unity is the key to overcoming obstacles.

Activity 2

Collaborative Puzzle Creation

Readers understand the creative process behind crafting engaging puzzles. Through actively constructing riddles, Luna, Buzz, and Princess Harmony experience the effort required to design challenges. This fosters an appreciation for the creators of puzzles, promoting empathy and recognizing the connection between creative expression and effective problem-solving.

Activity 3

Storytelling through Riddles

Readers explore the integration of riddles into storytelling, understanding that challenges can enhance narrative depth. Luna, Buzz, and Princess Harmony demonstrate that effective storytelling involves seamlessly weaving challenges into the plot. This activity promotes a holistic understanding of storytelling and problem-solving, emphasizing their synergistic relationship.

Activity 4

Mindful Meditation and Reflection

Readers grasp the importance of mindfulness and clarity in solving problems. Luna, Buzz, and Princess Harmony showcase that a calm and focused mind contributes to effective critical thinking. Through guided meditation and reflection, readers learn to cultivate self-awareness, reinforcing the idea that a clear mind is essential for tackling challenges.

Activity 5

Collaborative Art Project

Readers experience the synergy between art, teamwork, and critical thinking. Luna, Buzz, and Princess Harmony illustrate that collaborative efforts can result in visually compelling representations of complex ideas. This activity fosters an appreciation for diverse talents and perspectives in problem-solving, highlighting the value of creative collaboration.

Activity 6

Enchanted Forest Exploration

Readers connect with nature and realize that inspiration for critical thinking can come from the world around them. Luna, Buzz, and Princess Harmony demonstrate the importance of curiosity and observation in problem-solving. This activity encourages readers to explore their surroundings, fostering a sense of wonder and curiosity as they navigate challenges.

Activity 7

Virtual Escape Room Challenge

Readers adapt problem-solving skills to a virtual environment, realizing the versatility of critical thinking. Luna, Buzz, and Princess Harmony demonstrate that challenges can manifest in various forms, preparing readers to approach problem-solving with flexibility and adaptability. This activity introduces the concept that virtual collaboration is a valuable skill in navigating contemporary challenges.

Chapter 15

The Great Leadership Bake-Off
****

A day in the heart of the Enchanted Forest, Luna the Wise Owl, Buzz the Brave Little Bee, and Princess Harmony found themselves in a whimsical meadow filled with the sweet aroma of adventure. The magic of the forest stirred, and soon, a messenger bird descended, carrying ornate scrolls that bore the secrets to a legendary dessert known as the Harmony Delight.

The characters' eyes sparkled with curiosity as they unfurled the scrolls, revealing a series of enchanting illustrations that held the key to this magical culinary adventure. Luna, with her wisdom; Buzz, with his bravery; and Princess Harmony, with her regal charm, gathered beneath the shade of the Grand Baking Oak Tree to read the mystical recipes.

Their journey into the magical world of baking began with a laughter-filled collaboration. The characters worked together to decode the whimsical drawings and uncover the ingredients needed for Harmony Delight. From honey nectar to enchanted berries, each element had its place in the dessert, and the characters were eager to embark on their delicious quest.

As the mystery unfolded, Luna, Buzz, and Princess Harmony found themselves faced with a unique challenge—the collaborative mixing bowl. This enchanted bowl responded not only to ingredients but also to the synchronized movements of those who stirred its contents. It was a test of coordination and cooperation, requiring the characters to blend their strengths into a harmonious dance of creation.

Dividing themselves into teams, each led by one of the characters, the forest inhabitants joined Luna, Buzz, and Princess Harmony in the Great Leadership Bake-Off. Laughter echoed through the meadow as characters engaged in a synchronized ballet of baking, whisking, and folding. The collaborative mixing bowl responded to their united efforts, magically ensuring that only through teamwork could the perfect batter be achieved.

In the heart of the meadow, surrounded by the buzz of bees, the hoots of owls, and the laughter of forest creatures, the aroma of the baking dessert filled the air. The Great Leadership Bake-Off became not just a culinary adventure but a joyous celebration of teamwork, coordination, and the sweet essence of leadership.

As the first batch of Harmony Delight emerged from the enchanted ovens, Luna, Buzz, and Princess Harmony gathered the forest inhabitants around a grand table adorned with the magical dessert. Each character indulged in the sweet fruits of their collective labour, savouring the delicious harmony that filled their hearts.

The Great Leadership Bake-Off had come to an end, leaving behind not just the aroma of delightful treats but also important leadership insights. Luna, Buzz, and Princess Harmony shared the lessons learned with their forest companions, emphasizing the magic found in collaboration, coordination, and the beauty of diverse talents coming together.

As the sun dipped below the horizon, Luna, Buzz, and Princess Harmony looked at the starlit sky, grateful for the enchanting day they had shared. The Grand Baking Oak Tree stood as a witness to the friendships forged, the laughter shared, and the leadership lessons baked into the heart of the Enchanted Forest. And so, under the moon's gentle glow, Luna, Buzz, Princess Harmony, and their forest friends embraced the sweetness of their shared adventure, carrying the magic of collaboration into the next chapter of their enchanting journey.

But here is your chance to join them on this playful journey where you can get a chance to showcase your creativity with the Enchanted Forest!

Activity 1

Enchanted Recipe Scrolls

Invite the children to embark on their own magical baking adventure by creating Enchanted Recipe Scrolls. Provide each child with parchment paper, markers, and art supplies. Let them draw whimsical illustrations and write down the steps for their imaginary magical dessert. This activity not only sparks creativity but also introduces them to the concept of following instructions, a fundamental skill in baking.

Activity 2

Decorate Your Baking Apron

Enhance the baking experience by letting the children decorate their baking aprons. Provide plain aprons, fabric markers, stickers, and fabric paint. Encourage them to express their personalities and the theme of their magical dessert on the aprons. This creative outlet adds a personalized touch to their baking attire and builds excitement for the upcoming culinary adventure.

Activity 3

Ingredient Exploration

Create an interactive learning experience by setting up an "Ingredient Exploration" station. Lay out bowls with various safe and edible ingredients (flour, sugar, berries, etc.) that represent the magical elements found in the Enchanted Forest. Allow the children to touch, smell, and explore the ingredients, fostering a sensory connection and introducing them to basic baking components.

Activity 4

Enchanted Mixing Bowl Craft

Encourage teamwork and coordination with an Enchanted Mixing Bowl Craft. Provide materials such as paper plates, paint, glitter, and ribbon. Instruct the children to decorate their magical mixing bowls, emphasizing the importance of working together to create a harmonious design. This activity reinforces the collaborative spirit central to the baking adventure.

Activity 5

Cupcake Castle Decorating

Extend the magical theme by incorporating a Cupcake Castle Decorating activity. Bake cupcakes in advance and provide various frosting colors, edible decorations, and small castle-themed toppers. Each child can decorate their cupcake, turning it into a delicious castle masterpiece. This activity adds an extra layer of enchantment to the baking journey and allows for individual creativity.

Activity 6

Baking Ballet

Transform the act of stirring and mixing into a delightful Baking Ballet. Play music and encourage the children to dance and move in a synchronized manner as they take turns stirring their imaginary enchanted mixing bowls. This activity not only adds a playful element but also reinforces the idea of coordination and cooperation in the baking process.

Activity 7

Magical Cookie Cutter Adventure

Incorporate a Magical Cookie Cutter Adventure by providing an array of enchanting cookie cutters related to the Enchanted Forest theme. Let the children cut out cookies from rolled dough, turning them into magical shapes. This hands-on activity enhances fine motor skills and allows them to witness the transformation of dough into whimsical treats.

Activity 8

Forest Creature Cupcake Toppers

Extend the magical atmosphere by crafting Forest Creature Cupcake Toppers. Supply materials such as coloured paper, markers, and toothpicks. Instruct the children to create their favourite Enchanted Forest creatures to adorn their cupcakes. This artistic endeavour adds a personal touch to their baked creations and reinforces the theme of the enchanted journey.

Activity 9

Baking Story Circle

Conclude the baking activities with a Baking Story Circle. Gather the children around and encourage each one to share a magical story related to their dessert creation. This storytelling session allows them to express their creativity, share their experiences, and build camaraderie in the enchanted kitchen.

Activity 10

Dessert Display and Celebration

Transform the culmination of the baking adventure into a Dessert Display and Celebration. Set up a visually appealing display of the children's baked goods. Create a celebratory atmosphere by incorporating decorations, music, and a shared appreciation for the magical desserts. This final activity not only showcases their culinary creations but also reinforces the joy of collaboration and the sweetness found in shared accomplishments.

Lesson Learned

***

Activity 1

Enchanted Recipe Scrolls

In this engaging activity, children will experience the magical journey by receiving Enchanted Recipe Scrolls. The scrolls, filled with whimsical illustrations, discover the secrets to a legendary dessert named the Harmony Delight. Children eagerly unfurl the scrolls, their eyes sparkling with curiosity, as they discover the enchanting drawings that hold the key to this mystical culinary adventure. This activity not only introduces them to the joy of baking but also initiates an understanding of the sequential nature of recipes.

Activity 2

Decorate Your Baking Apron

Children express their individuality and creativity by decorating their baking aprons. This hands-on craft activity fosters a sense of personalization and uniqueness. By creating their designs, children learn that while collaboration is essential, each person brings a special touch to the collaborative effort, celebrating individuality within a team.

Activity 3

Ingredient Exploration

The Ingredient Exploration activity transforms the kitchen into a magical laboratory. Children get hands-on experience with various baking ingredients, fostering curiosity about the diverse elements contributing to a delightful treat. This activity lays the groundwork for understanding the basics of recipes and introduces them to the concept of combining ingredients.

Activity 4

Enchanted Mixing Bowl Craft

Crafting the Enchanted Mixing Bowl becomes a group effort, promoting teamwork and coordination. Children learn the value of working together towards a common goal, emphasizing that combining individual efforts can lead to a harmonious and visually appealing result. This collaborative craft introduces them to the idea that teamwork enhances the overall experience.

Activity 5

Cupcake Castle Decorating

Children enter the world of edible artistry by decorating cupcake castles. This activity merges the deliciousness of baking with the creativity of artistic expression. Each child gets the opportunity to showcase their unique style, reinforcing the idea that baking can be both a delectable and imaginative endeavour.

Activity 6

Baking Ballet

The Baking Ballet transforms the act of baking into a synchronized dance. Children engage in coordinated movements, turning routine tasks into a playful and harmonious activity. This not only brings joy to the baking process but also emphasizes the importance of teamwork in the kitchen.

Activity 7

Magical Cookie Cutter Adventure

Children explore the transformative aspect of baking by using magical cookie cutters. This hands-on activity enhances fine motor skills as they create cookies with whimsical shapes. It teaches them that even the simplest piece of dough can become something delightful and enchanting.

Activity 8

Forest Creature Cupcake Toppers

Crafting cupcake toppers adds a personal touch to their creations. Children engage in a creative process that reinforces the idea that every detail matters. They learn that individual contributions, no matter how small, enhance the overall enchanting experience of baking.

Activity 9

Baking Story Circle

The Baking Story Circle encourages children to articulate their thoughts and experiences related to the baking adventure. This activity fosters communication skills as each child shares their unique story. It promotes a sense of community, reinforcing the joy of collaboration and creating a shared narrative.

Activity 10

Dessert Display and Celebration

Concluding the enchanting day with a Dessert Display and Celebration, children learn the importance of recognizing and celebrating shared accomplishments. They take pride in their collaborative efforts and understand that the joy of baking extends beyond the kitchen to be shared with others. This activity reinforces the idea that the sweetness of success is best enjoyed together.

Chapter 16

Diversity Costume

***

Luna the Wise Owl, Buzz the Brave Little Bee, and Princess Harmony stumbled upon a hidden clearing illuminated by the soft glow of magical fireflies. As they offered further, the air crackled with anticipation, and the trees whispered secrets of an extraordinary chapter awaiting them.

At the centre of the clearing stood the Luminary Oak, a majestic tree adorned with a myriad of lanterns that emitted a dazzling array of colours. The branches of the tree reached out like embracing arms, and beneath its radiant glow lay an array of vibrant fabrics, ribbons, and sparkling accessories.

The Luminary Oak spoke in a voice that seemed to resonate from the very heart of the forest,

"Welcome, dear friends. Today, you shall embark on a journey of diversity and unity. Each of you shall weave a costume that represents your unique essence, and together, you shall create a tapestry that celebrates the beauty of differences."

Intrigued and enchanted, Luna, Buzz, and Princess Harmony approached the Luminary Oak, their eyes reflecting the spark of curiosity.

"What a wondrous idea," Luna remarked with a twinkle in her wise eyes. Buzz buzzed with excitement, "I've never crafted a costume before!"

Princess Harmony, with regal grace, nodded in agreement, "Let us start this artistic journey together."

The clearing echoed with laughter as Luna, Buzz, and Princess Harmony explored the vibrant fabrics, each drawn to those that resonated with their personalities. Luna chose deep blues and purples, representing the wisdom of the night sky.

Buzz flitted around in vibrant yellows and greens, mirroring the adventurous hues of the Enchanted Forest. Princess Harmony draped herself in regal reds and golds, embodying the harmonious connection she felt with all beings.

As the characters immersed themselves in the art of costume crafting, the Luminary Oak's magical influence became apparent. The fabrics seemed to respond to their touch, transforming into a living canvas adorned with intricate patterns that intertwined, symbolizing the interconnectedness of their stories.

"Let us share our tales as we weave these fabrics together," suggested Luna, her eyes gleaming with wisdom.

Buzz eagerly chimed in, "I once ventured into the Meadow of Whispers to retrieve pollen for the Queen Bee!"

Princess Harmony added with grace, "In my realm, we celebrate the symphony of all living beings."

Collaboratively, Luna, Buzz, and Princess Harmony began sewing, braiding, and embellishing their costumes. As they worked, they shared stories of their journeys, discovering common threads that wove them together. Luna's wisdom complemented Buzz's bravery, and Princess Harmony's regality tied their stories into a harmonious tapestry.

The Luminary Oak observed with benevolent delight as the characters celebrated their uniqueness while embracing the common threads that bound them. Lanterns above flickered with approval, casting a warm light on their collaborative masterpiece.

As the final stitches were placed, Luna, Buzz, and Princess Harmony stood together in a circle, each wearing a costume that embodied not only their strengths but also the beauty of their unity.

The Luminary Oak whispered, "In diversity, you find strength. In unity, you discover the true magic of connection."

The characters felt a profound sense of belonging, realizing that their differences were not only accepted but celebrated. The Luminary Oak's words had become a mantra, resonating with the forest inhabitants who had gathered to witness the enchanting transformation.

Under the Luminary Oak's radiant branches, Luna, Buzz, Princess Harmony, and the entire forest felt a deep sense of unity, understanding that diversity was the enchanting thread binding them together in the ever-evolving tapestry of the Enchanted Forest. And as the moon rose, casting its gentle light upon the clearing, the Luminary Oak stood as evidence of the beauty found in the acceptance of diversity and the celebration of shared experiences. But here is your chance to join them on this playful journey where you can get a chance to showcase your creativity with the Enchanted Forest!

Activity 1

Diversity Collage

Take a roll on the creative journey by inviting readers to create their own Diversity Collage. Provide them with a variety of colourful materials such as magazines, fabric scraps, and art supplies. Encourage them to select elements that resonate with their individuality. As they craft their collages, they prompt readers to reflect on the diverse aspects of their personalities, celebrating the unique qualities that make them who they are. This artistic effort serves as a tangible representation of the beauty found in embracing differences.

Activity 2

Unity Bracelet Making

Introduce the concept of unity through a hands-on experience of bracelet making. Supply readers with an assortment of beads, each representing a different aspect of diversity. As they thread the beads onto a string, guide them to consider the connection of each bead in creating a harmonious bracelet. Encourage reflection on how the varied beads symbolize the diverse yet interconnected elements that contribute to the overall unity of the Enchanted Forest.

Activity 4

Collaborative Art Mural

Transform the reading experience into a collaborative art project by creating a Diversity Mural. Provide readers with a large canvas or mural paper, along with art supplies. Prompt them to contribute individual artworks that celebrate diversity and unity. As each reader adds their piece to the mural, they actively participate in the creation of a visual representation of the interconnected stories within the Enchanted Forest.

Activity 5

Cultural Exchange Journal

Encourage readers to start on a Cultural Exchange Journal activity. Invite them to explore and document aspects of their own culture or traditions, as well as those of others. Through writing, drawing, or collaging, readers can share and celebrate the richness of diverse cultures. This activity promotes awareness, understanding, and a sense of unity among readers as they exchange insights into their unique cultural backgrounds.

Activity 6

Diversity Book Club

Establish a Diversity Book Club where readers can explore literature that celebrates diversity and unity. Select books that showcase characters from various backgrounds and experiences. After reading, encourage discussions that highlight the importance of implementation differences and finding common ground. This activity not only promotes a love for reading but also raises meaningful conversations about diversity and unity.

Lessons Learned

***

Activity 1

Diversity Collage

In creating their Diversity Collage, readers learn the valuable lesson that each individual is a unique mosaic of experiences, interests, and characteristics. This activity emphasizes the beauty found in embracing one's individuality and appreciating the diversity that collectively forms a vibrant community.

Activity 2

Unity Bracelet Making

Through the Unity Bracelet Making activity, readers grasp the significance of interconnectedness and unity. The lesson learned is that, much like the beads on the bracelet, the diverse elements within a community contribute to a harmonious whole. Each bead symbolizes a unique aspect, and together, they create a stronger, more resilient bond.

Activity 3

Personal Storytelling Circle

Participating in the Personal Storytelling Circle teaches readers the power of empathy and understanding. By sharing and actively listening to diverse stories, readers recognize the importance of acknowledging and respecting the varied experiences that shape individuals. This activity fosters a sense of connection and shared humanity.

Activity 4

Collaborative Art Mural

In contributing to the creation of a Collaborative Art Mural, readers learn the lesson of collective creativity and the strength derived from diverse perspectives. This activity emphasizes that when individuals come together, each offering their unique artistic expression, they contribute to the beauty of a larger, more inclusive narrative.

Activity 5

Cultural Exchange Journal

Engaging in the Cultural Exchange Journal activity provides readers with the lesson of cultural appreciation and understanding. By documenting and sharing aspects of their own culture and learning about others, readers recognize the richness that diversity brings to the community. This activity promotes a sense of openness and respect for different cultural backgrounds.

Activity 9

Diversity Book Club

Participating in the Diversity Book Club encourages readers to appreciate diverse narratives and perspectives. The lesson learned is that literature has the power to broaden understanding and promote empathy. This activity fosters a love for reading while reinforcing the idea that diverse stories contribute to a more enriched collective narrative.

Chapter **17**

Leadership in Action
***

Luna the Wise Owl, Buzz the Brave Little Bee, and Princess Harmony gathered beneath the ancient Wisdom Willow, and a profound excitement filled the air. Their enchanting journey, marked by whimsical adventures and meaningful lessons, had led them to a mysterious clearing, a stage adorned with symbols representing the essence of their leadership journey.

As Luna perched on a wisdom-inspired branch, Buzz buzzed with an energetic hum, and Princess Harmony gracefully approached the magical podium; the forest seemed to hold its breath. The instruments before them, enchanted and attuned to the frequencies of leadership, humor, creativity, and unity, awaited the characters' touch.

Luna, with her eyes gleaming with wisdom, began, "Let us embark on this Leadership Symphony, where our individual notes combine to create a melody that resonates through the Enchanted Forest."

Buzz joined in with a playful buzz, "A masterpiece that reflects our journey of unity, creativity, humor, and leadership!"

Princess Harmony, adorned in her regal attire, added, "May the music of our actions inspire and enchant every corner of our beloved forest."

The first movement, "Harmony of Unity," unfolded with Luna composing the dance of their collective strengths. Luna's deep insights, Buzz's daring maneuvers, and Princess Harmony's elegant moves created a harmonious ballet, symbolizing the strength derived from embracing diversity.

In the midst of the dance, Luna remarked, "In unity, we find the strength to weather any storm. Each note, unique in its own right, contributes to the symphony of our community."

As the characters moved to the second movement, "Crescendo of Creativity," they deep themselves in a vibrant art display. Luna's brush strokes reflected the wisdom of ages, Buzz crafted unusual sculptures with finesse, and Princess Harmony added grace to the canvas with her regal touch.

Buzz, buzzing with excitement, declared, "Our forest is more colorful when every note contributes to the masterpiece."

The third movement, "Jubilant Humor," saw Luna, Buzz, and Princess Harmony engaged in playful banter and laughter. Luna's wise quips echoed, Buzz's cheerful buzzing added a lively rhythm, and Princess Harmony's jests brought a sense of lightness to the masterpiece.

Princess Harmony laughed and said, "In the laughter shared among us, we find the magic that binds us together. Humor is the bridge that connects hearts."

The grand finale, "Leadership Crescendo," witnessed Luna, Buzz, and Princess Harmony standing united, each wearing a crown symbolizing their unique leadership qualities. The enchanted instruments swirled around them, creating a melody that reflected the positive impact of their leadership on the Enchanted Forest.

Luna, looking at her friends, remarked,

"Our journey has been a melody, and each of you has played a crucial role in composing the Leadership Symphony. May our forest always resonate with the tunes of unity, creativity, humor, and effective leadership."

As the last notes faded away, the Enchanted Forest seemed to glow with newfound enchantment. Luna, Buzz, and Princess Harmony stood together, surrounded by the magical echoes of their collective journey. The grand finale not only celebrated their growth and leadership qualities but also left an indelible mark on the heart of the Enchanted Forest. But here is your chance to join them on this playful journey where you can get a chance to showcase your creativity with the Enchanted Forest!

Activity 1

Leadership Crown Crafting

Provide materials like colorful paper, stickers, markers, and glitter for Leadership Crown Crafting. Guide readers in designing their own crowns, encouraging them to include symbols or words that represent their unique leadership qualities related to unity, creativity, humor, and effective leadership. After completing the crowns, initiate a celebratory ceremony where each reader wears their creation proudly, embodying the leadership lessons learned from Luna, Buzz, and Princess Harmony.

Activity 2

Collaborative Storytelling

Organize a Collaborative Storytelling session where readers contribute to an ongoing narrative. The story should incorporate themes of unity, creativity, humor, and effective leadership, drawing inspiration from the adventures of Luna, Buzz, and Princess Harmony. Each reader adds a paragraph or chapter, building upon the contributions of others. This activity not only fosters creativity but also emphasizes the power of collaboration in storytelling.

Activity 3

Musical Instrument Craft

Encourage readers to create their own magical musical instruments using materials like cardboard, strings, and colorful decorations. The instruments should represent the enchanted elements of unity, creativity, humor, and effective leadership. After crafting their instruments, readers can participate in a mini-musical performance, expressing their understanding of the leadership masterpiece through the magical tunes of their creations.

Lessons Learned

***

Activity 1

Leadership Crown Crafting

As readers design their Leadership Crowns, they discover the lesson that effective leadership is a source of pride and empowerment. The act of creating a crown with symbols representing unity, creativity, humor, and effective leadership instills a sense of ownership and celebration of their unique qualities. Wearing the crowns becomes a tangible reminder of their growth and leadership capabilities. This activity fosters self-confidence and emphasizes the idea that embracing one's leadership qualities is a cause for celebration.

Activity 2

Collaborative Storytelling

In participating in Collaborative Storytelling, readers hold the significance of teamwork in creating a consistent and engaging narrative. The knitting together of various ideas reflects the power of collaboration, showcasing how diverse perspectives contribute to a richer and more imaginative story. This activity underscores the lesson that effective leadership involves not only individual creativity but also the ability to collaborate impeccably with others to create something greater than the sum of its parts.

Activity 3

Musical Instrument Craft

Creating magical musical instruments imparts the lesson that effective leadership is an art that can be expressed in various forms. Each instrument, representing unity, creativity, humor, and effective leadership, serves as a unique contribution to the leadership kingdom. Readers understand that leadership is not a one-size-fits-all concept; rather, it can be expressed in diverse ways. This activity encourages readers to find their own leadership "tune" and appreciate the beauty of leadership diversity.

Chapter **18**

The Magic within You
***

Luna the Wise Owl, Buzz the Brave Little Bee, and Princess Harmony stumbled upon a hidden grove bathed in the soft glow of magical fireflies. Intrigued, they entered the grove and immediately felt a sense of serenity and anticipation. The air was filled with the sweet scent of blooming flowers, and the trees swayed gently as if inviting the trio into a sacred space.

As Luna, Buzz, and Princess Harmony ventured further, the atmosphere changed, and the magical aura intensified. Suddenly, a mystical figure materialized before them. It was a guardian spirit of the Enchanted Forest, a being woven from the very essence of nature. The spirit greeted Luna, Buzz, and Princess Harmony with a knowing smile, acknowledging their presence in this sacred space.

The spirit, with an air of wisdom, revealed the true nature of the grove—it was a place of self-discovery and empowerment, where characters and readers alike would unlock the dormant potential of their leadership. Luna, Buzz, and Princess Harmony were bestowed with enchanted tokens, each representing a unique aspect of their leadership strengths.

Luna's token was a shimmering feather, a symbol of wisdom that glistened with the accumulated knowledge of the ages. Buzz received a radiant sunflower, representing bravery and resilience, while Princess Harmony's token was a sparkling tiara, embodying regal charm and the ability to unite. These tokens, the spirit explained, were not just trinkets but conduits of inner magic, constant reminders of the characters' latent potential.

Emboldened by their enchanted tokens, Luna, Buzz, and Princess Harmony embarked on a transformative journey within the grove. The air echoed with their laughter and the rustle of leaves as they shared personal stories of leadership, triumphs, and growth. The characters discovered the unique qualities that set them apart and the collective strength that bound them together.

In a moment of profound invitation, the guardian spirit encouraged the readers to join Luna, Buzz, and Princess Harmony in unlocking their own leadership potential. Readers became active participants in the unfolding narrative, discovering the strength within themselves and finding the courage to share their experiences with the broader community.

Under the ancient, wise trees, a storytelling circle emerged—a gathering where characters and readers alike exchanged tales of overcoming challenges, demonstrating resilience, and embracing their individuality. The collective learning environment flourished, with each story weaving into the tapestry of inspiration that resonated through the Enchanted Forest.

As the enchanted fireflies wove intricate patterns of light in the gathering dusk, Luna, Buzz, Princess Harmony, and the readers realized that the true magic of leadership lay not in grand gestures but in the authentic sharing of one's journey. The Enchanted Forest, with its mystical grove, had become a catalyst for unlocking the leadership potential within every individual.

In the closing whispers of the breeze, the guardian spirit commended Luna, Buzz, Princess Harmony, and the readers for embracing their inner magic. The enchanted tokens, now aglow with luminous light, symbolized not just individual strengths but the interconnected brilliance of a community united in their leadership journey.

And so, under the starlit sky, Luna, Buzz, Princess Harmony, and the readers continued to share their stories. The guardian spirit stood as a silent witness, and the enchanted grove remained a timeless sanctuary—a place where the magic within each character and reader converged, creating an enduring legacy of empowerment and celebration in the heart of the Enchanted Forest.

Activity 1

Leadership Tokens Craft

Gather art supplies such as colour paper, markers, glue, and glitter. Encourage kids to create their enchanted leadership tokens. Each child can choose an animal or nature-inspired token that represents a specific leadership quality. For example, a wise owl for wisdom, a brave bee for courage, or a tiara for unity. Discuss the chosen qualities and have kids share why they associate them with leadership. This activity not only sparks creativity but also allows children to reflect on essential leadership traits.

Activity 2

Storytelling Circle

Create a cosy storytelling corner with blankets and cushions. Provide a magical prop, like a glowing orb or a fairy light, to set the atmosphere. Encourage kids to share their own leadership stories or create imaginative tales inspired by Luna the Wise Owl, Buzz the Brave Little Bee, and Princess Harmony. This activity promotes verbal expression, creativity, and active listening, fostering a sense of community among the young storytellers.

Activity 3

Nature Scavenger Hunt

Organize a nature scavenger hunt in a local park or wooded area. Provide kids with a list of items related to leadership qualities—such as a strong rock symbolizing resilience or a vibrant leaf representing growth. As they find each item, discuss how it connects to leadership. This outdoor activity combines the benefits of nature exploration with the concept of leadership, encouraging kids to appreciate the qualities found in the world around them.

Activity 4

Magic Mirror Affirmations

Provide small mirrors and art supplies like stickers, markers, and gems. Ask kids to decorate their mirrors with positive affirmations related to leadership. Encourage them to stand in front of their mirrors, look themselves in the eyes, and recite their chosen affirmations. This activity promotes self-confidence, self-reflection, and the understanding that leadership begins with believing in oneself.

Activity 5

Enchanted Forest Dance Party

Create a playlist with music inspired by the Enchanted Forest theme. Have a dance party where kids can express themselves through movement. Encourage them to dance freely, embodying the leadership qualities of Luna, Buzz, and Princess Harmony. This activity not only provides a fun outlet for energy but also reinforces the idea that leadership can be joyful and expressive.

Activity 6

Leadership Role-Playing

Prepare simple scripts or scenarios that involve leadership challenges. Assign roles to kids, allowing them to step into the shoes of Luna, Buzz, or Princess Harmony. Through role-playing, children can explore decision-making, communication, and problem-solving skills. This interactive activity helps them understand leadership dynamics playfully and engagingly.

Activity 7

Magical Story Stones Creation

Collect smooth stones and art supplies like markers or paint. Ask kids to illustrate characters or symbols representing leadership qualities on the stones. Once finished, they can use these enchanted story stones to create collaborative narratives, incorporating the leadership traits depicted. This storytelling activity fosters creativity, cooperation, and communication skills.

Lessons Learned

***

Activity 1

Leadership Tokens Craft

Children, through crafting their enchanted leadership tokens, learn to associate qualities like wisdom, courage, and unity with tangible symbols. This activity sparks creativity while encouraging reflection on essential leadership traits. By discussing their chosen qualities, kids not only express themselves artistically but also engage in thoughtful conversations, fostering an early understanding of the diverse aspects of effective leadership.

Activity 2

Storytelling Circle

The storytelling circle promotes verbal expression, creativity, and active listening. As kids share their leadership stories inspired by forest characters, they learn the art of storytelling and communication. This activity creates a sense of community among the young storytellers, fostering an understanding that leadership involves sharing experiences and ideas in a supportive environment.

Activity 3

Nature Scavenger Hunt

Engaging in a nature scavenger hunt connects leadership qualities with elements found in the natural world. By associating items like a strong rock or a vibrant leaf with resilience and growth, children learn to appreciate and apply leadership traits in various contexts. This outdoor activity not only encourages exploration but also instills a deeper connection between leadership and the world around them.

Activity 4

Magic Mirror Affirmations

Through decorating mirrors with positive affirmations related to leadership, kids gain a valuable lesson in self-confidence and self-reflection. Encouraging them to recite affirmations while looking into their mirrors reinforces the idea that leadership begins with believing in oneself. This activity contributes to building a positive self-image and cultivating the inner strength necessary for effective leadership.

Activity 5

Enchanted Forest Dance Party

The dance party reinforces the idea that leadership can be joyful and expressive. By embodying the leadership qualities of Luna, Buzz, and Princess Harmony through movement, children learn that effective leadership can be dynamic and fun. This activity encourages them to express themselves physically and emotionally, understanding that leadership is not limited to serious or formal contexts.

Activity 6

Leadership Role-Playing

Through role-playing scenarios involving leadership challenges, children explore decision-making, communication, and problem-solving skills playfully and engagingly. This interactive activity helps them understand leadership dynamics early on, fostering critical thinking and collaboration. By stepping into the shoes of forest characters, kids gain insights into various leadership styles and approaches.

Activity 7

Magical Story Stones Creation

The creation of enchanted story stones fosters creativity, cooperation, and communication skills. By illustrating characters or symbols representing leadership qualities, children contribute to collaborative narratives. This storytelling activity promotes the understanding that leadership involves weaving together diverse strengths to create a cohesive and engaging story. The stones become tangible reminders of the importance of teamwork and imagination in leadership.

Chapter **19**

The Takeaways
***

As we journey through the enchanted pages of 'Leadership Lullabies,' the understanding of leadership unfolds with whimsy and wisdom. Each chapter has woven lessons, like threads of magic, into the hearts of Luna, Buzz, Princess Harmony, and our cherished readers. Now, as we stand at the threshold of reflection, let us delve into the enchanted reservoir of takeaways—nuggets of insight and wisdom that sparkle like stardust in the forest of leadership development.

Part I:
Bedtime Stories for
Growing Great Leaders

Chapter 1

The Adventure Begins

In the opening chapter, readers are introduced to Luna, the Wise Owl, who becomes a guide for young minds on their journey of leadership development. Luna's story emphasizes the importance of wisdom and attentive listening in leadership. The narrative unfolds with Luna and other characters collaborating to solve a puzzle, showcasing the value of shared knowledge and cooperation in achieving common goals.

Chapter 2

The Brave Little Bee

This chapter revolves around Buzz, the Brave Little Bee, and his journey in the Golden Meadows. The narrative underscores the significance of courage and resilience in leadership. Buzz's character confronts and overcomes challenges, becoming a metaphor for the obstacles leaders may face. The story inspires young readers to face the unknown with bravery and determination, reinforcing the idea that overcoming fears is an essential aspect of leadership.

Chapter 3

Princess Harmony and the Kingdom of Empathy

Princess Harmony takes center stage in this chapter, where her character represents the transformative power of empathy in leadership. The enchanted kingdom within the forest becomes a magical backdrop, emphasizing empathy as the guiding principle. Harmony's act of gifting heart-shaped pendants to each character symbolizes their connection through empathy, portraying the profound impact empathy can have on leadership dynamics.

Chapter 4

The Kindness Castle

Kindness becomes the focal point in this chapter, using the metaphor of a Kindness Castle to explore the role of kindness in leadership. The magical elements and characters contribute to a whimsical and engaging narrative, making the concept of kindness accessible and memorable for young readers. The bestowal of kindness crowns upon characters and highlights the inspiration and compassion that kindness brings to leadership roles.

Chapter 5

Sir Determination and the Dragon of Challenges

Sir Determination takes the spotlight in this chapter, embodying the importance of perseverance and resilience in leadership. The dragon serves as a metaphor for life's challenges, and the triumph over them becomes a powerful lesson for young readers about overcoming difficulties with determination and a positive mindset. The narrative encourages resilience as a key leadership trait, fostering the understanding that challenges are growth opportunities.

Chapter 6

The Magical Mirror of Self-Reflection

The enchanted mirror becomes a magical tool in this chapter, conveying the importance of self-reflection and self-awareness in leadership. By exploring the characters' inner worlds, the story inspires young readers to understand and accept themselves, laying the foundation for personal and leadership growth. The mirror's ability to reflect not just physical appearances but also the characters' inner thoughts and emotions adds depth to the narrative.

Chapter 7

The Giggle Goblins' Lesson

Humor and positivity take center stage with the introduction of the Giggle Goblins – Giggly, Chuckle, and Snicker. These characters infuse laughter into the Enchanted Forest, illustrating the value of maintaining a positive attitude in leadership roles. The playful challenges and magical elements contribute to a lighthearted and engaging narrative, leaving young readers with the understanding that a positive outlook can be a powerful asset in leadership.

Chapter 8

King Creativity's Canvas

Creativity and innovation come to life in King Creativity's workshop, where characters learn the importance of a supportive environment for nurturing creativity. King Creativity awards each character a creative crown, symbolizing their potential as innovative leaders. The characters' realization of their creative capabilities emphasizes the importance of embracing imaginative thinking in leadership. The magical elements of the Kingdom of Imagination convey the idea that creativity is a valuable aspect of effective leadership.

Chapter 9

Captain Curiosity's Quest

The adventurous explorer, Captain Curiosity, takes young readers on a quest for knowledge in this chapter. The magical cove filled with books, maps, and artifacts sparks curiosity and emphasizes the joy and value of continuous learning in leadership. Captain Curiosity's character encourages readers to appreciate the importance of curiosity in leadership roles, fostering a love for exploration and discovery.

Part II:
Games and Activities for
Kid Leadership Development

Chapter **10**

Leadership Treasure Hunt

The concept of a Leadership Treasure Hunt is introduced, where characters embark on an outdoor adventure to discover hidden enchanted clues. Characters receive a magical map revealing the locations of challenges scattered throughout the Enchanted Forest. This outdoor problem-solving activity becomes an engaging and interactive way for characters to learn and apply essential leadership skills. The diverse challenges and collaborative elements make the Treasure Hunt an exciting and memorable part of the overall narrative, reinforcing the idea that leadership development can be an adventurous journey.

Chapter 11

Storyboard Leadership

A magical tree becomes a symbol of personal and leadership growth in this chapter. Each character's story contributes to the blossoming of the tree's vibrant leaves, highlighting the interconnectedness of their experiences. Characters receive magical sketchbooks that come to life as they sketch and narrate their leadership stories, emphasizing the uniqueness of each character's journey. The chapter fosters creativity, self-expression, and reflection, providing young readers with a tangible representation of their personal and leadership development.

Chapter 12

Building a Kindness Kingdom

In this chapter, characters collaborate to construct a magical tree sculpture symbolizing the growth of friendship and kindness in their shared space. Each leaf or ornament on the tree represents an act of kindness contributed by a character. The use of arts and crafts as a medium for expressing and reinforcing positive values creates a whimsical and engaging narrative. The magical and enchanting elements of the project inspire readers to incorporate kindness into their collaborative endeavors, promoting the idea that leadership can be grounded in compassion and goodwill.

Chapter 13

Superhero Leadership Capes

Characters recite a superhero alliance oath, pledging to use their leadership capes for the greater good and to inspire positive change. The chapter highlights the characters' commitment to embodying their chosen leadership qualities through crafting, turning the act into a magical and empowering experience. Characters design capes that embody their unique strengths, and the collaborative elements contribute to a narrative that encourages readers to explore and celebrate their own leadership qualities creatively and imaginatively. The symbolism of the capes reinforces the idea that everyone possesses leadership potential.

Chapter 14

Leader's Puzzle Palace

Characters enter a chamber filled with riddles that require critical thinking to solve. The chapter showcases the characters collaborating and using their collective intelligence to unravel the challenging riddles. The emphasis on critical thinking and collaboration provides a playful yet educational approach to developing problem-solving skills in young readers. The narrative encourages the idea that effective leadership involves a combination of intellect, teamwork, and creative problem-solving.

Chapter 15

The Great Leadership Bake-Off

The Great Leadership Bake-Off unfolds as characters receive mystery recipe scrolls unveiling the ingredients and steps for a magical dessert. The characters' curiosity and collaboration shine as they decipher the scrolls together. Teams use a collaborative mixing bowl that requires synchronized movements to create the perfect batter, highlighting the importance of coordination and cooperation in teamwork. The baking process becomes a memorable experience that not only satisfies the characters' sweet cravings but also leaves them with important leadership insights. The chapter illustrates that effective leadership involves teamwork, coordination, and the joy of shared accomplishments.

Chapter 16

Diversity Costume

This chapter utilizes the metaphor of a costume to convey the beauty and interconnectedness of diversity. Through collaborative artistry, characters celebrate their individuality and shared experiences, fostering a sense of unity and acceptance within the Enchanted Forest. The narrative encourages readers to appreciate and embrace diversity, recognizing that everyone contributes uniquely to the collective tapestry of leadership. The celebration of individuality and unity becomes a powerful lesson in leadership, promoting an inclusive and supportive community.

Chapter 17

Leadership in Action

The grand finale weaves together diverse elements of leadership, humor, creativity, and unity into a harmonious narrative. The characters' growth and the positive impact of effective leadership on the Enchanted Forest community are showcased. The chapter serves as a culmination of the leadership journey, illustrating the transformative power of leadership in action. Through a series of adventures and lessons, characters evolve into capable leaders who contribute positively to their community. The narrative encourages readers to recognize the multifaceted nature of leadership and its potential to bring about positive change.

Chapter 18

The Magic within You

Characters and readers are reminded of the magic within themselves, acknowledging that the Enchanted Forest was a catalyst for unlocking their leadership potential. The chapter illustrates the characters' and readers' newfound confidence in their abilities, emphasizing the idea that leadership is an inherent quality that can be nurtured and developed. Readers are encouraged to embrace their unique strengths and recognize the leadership potential within, fostering a sense of self-belief and empowerment.

Chapter 20

Acknowledgments and Gratitude

****

In this final chapter, the characters come together to express their deep gratitude for the meaningful leadership journey they experienced together in the Enchanted Forest. They thank each other for their partnership, support, creativity and diverse skills that enriched each story and activity. The characters also offer appreciation to the young readers for embarking on this magical adventure with them. They acknowledge that none of the inspiring tales or important leadership lessons would have been possible without a collaborative effort.

This chapter serves as a reflective conclusion, with the characters reminiscing on all they have learned about themselves and each other through the ups and downs of their journey. They recognize that leadership development is an ongoing process that requires continuous growth. To honor the new understandings they have gained, the characters pledge to keep nurturing their strengths while also welcoming new challenges. Finally, they encourage the readers to reflect on how they can apply leadership lessons in their own lives and communities. Just as the character's story is not truly finished, the readers are reminded that their potential as leaders has only begun to blossom.

This story serves as a lesson for all the members of the enchanted forest where they were all together to play their role in understanding and teaching the lessons of leadership, bringing all the creatures under the enchanted forest where they would love, teach, progress, and brought forward harmonious lessons that made the readers more efficient.

As the final chapter of "Leadership Lullabies" unfolded, it began with a heartfelt expression of gratitude, a tender acknowledgment of the characters and readers who had embarked on the enchanting leadership adventure within the pages of the book. The words, infused with sincerity, conveyed a profound appreciation for the companionship of Luna, the Wise Owl, Buzz, the Brave Little Bee, and Princess Harmony, recognizing them not just as fictional characters but as guiding lights illuminating the path toward leadership wisdom.

The narrative gracefully transitioned to extend gratitude to the readers, recognizing them as essential participants in this shared journey. The young minds that absorbed the tales and contemplated the lessons were acknowledged for their curiosity, imagination, and willingness to embrace the values of leadership woven into the fabric of the Enchanted Forest. The appreciation was not only for turning pages but for embracing the essence of leadership with open hearts and inquisitive minds.

In a touching moment, the chapter paid tribute to the collaborative effort that birthed the entire enchanting narrative. It was an acknowledgment of the collective creativity and dedication that went into crafting a story that not only entertained but also served as a beacon for leadership exploration. Authors, illustrators, and all contributors behind the scenes were recognized for their unique brushstrokes and words that breathed life into the magical realm, creating a symphony of storytelling.

As the narrative took a reflective turn, the concluding chapter served as more than just a farewell to a book—it became a reflective and inspirational conclusion to the leadership journey within the Enchanted Forest. It prompted characters and readers alike to pause and contemplate the transformative power of the tales they had woven together. The Enchanted Forest was not merely a setting; it was a metaphor for the boundless kingdom of leadership potential that extended beyond the pages.

Emphasizing the idea that leadership development is an ongoing process, the concluding paragraphs resonated with the belief that the journey was not confined to a book's boundaries. It was an encouragement for both characters and readers to continue their growth, applying the lessons learned within the enchanting tales to real-life situations. The Enchanted Forest, though bidding farewell as a tangible setting, remained alive in the hearts of all who had ventured through its mystical landscapes.

In its inspirational tone, the chapter closed with a call to action—an invitation for characters and readers to contribute positively to their communities. The Enchanted Forest's lessons were not meant to fade away but to be carried forward as a lantern illuminating the path of leadership in everyday life. It was a reminder that the story did not conclude with the final page turn; instead, it effortlessly merged into the ongoing narratives of characters and readers alike, ensuring that the magic of leadership would continue to thrive, grow, and inspire.

Thank You Readers

Dear Valued Readers,

As we reach the final chapter of "Leadership Lullabies," we find ourselves reflecting on the incredible journey we've shared within the Enchanted Forest. We extend our heartfelt gratitude to each of you for choosing this book and for allowing Luna the Wise Owl, Buzz the Brave Little Bee, and Princess Harmony to become cherished companions in your literary adventures.

Thank you for opening your hearts to the magic of storytelling and embracing the enchanting world we sought to create. Your curiosity, imagination, and commitment to exploring the realm of leadership within these pages have made this journey all the more meaningful.

As the characters bid farewell to the Enchanted Forest, we want to express our deepest appreciation for your company throughout this enchanting tale. Your presence has added warmth and vibrancy to the narrative, making every page come alive with the spirit of leadership, friendship, and growth.

In saying goodbye to this magical kingdom, we hope the lessons learned within the Enchanted Forest linger in your thoughts, inspiring your leadership adventures. May the wisdom of Luna, the courage of Buzz, and the empathy of Princess Harmony accompany you on your journey beyond these pages.

Thank you for being part of this extraordinary adventure. Your readership has been the magic that brought these tales to life.

With heartfelt gratitude,

Author Leadership Lullabies